Jerusalem: A Religious History

IqraSense.com

Other Books by IqraSense.com

1. Jesus – The Prophet Who Didn't Die
2. Summarized Stories of the Quran
3. The Power of Dua (Prayers)
4. Inspirations from the Quran - Selected DUAs, Verses, and Surahs from the Quran: Includes Select Commentary, Tafsir, and Reasons for Revelation
5. Healing and Shifa from the Quran and Sunnah
6. DUAs for Success
7. And more

Jerusalem: A Religious History

The centuries old Christian, Islamic, and Jewish struggle for the "Holy Lands"

IqraSense.com

Library of Congress Control Number: 2014920064
CreateSpace Independent Publishing Platform, North Charleston, SC

Printed in the United States of America

ISBN: 1503096084
ISBN-13:   978-1503096080

TABLE OF CONTENTS

This page is intentionally left blank.

1. Foreword

Jerusalem's history is special as well as fascinating for many reasons. First, Jerusalem is revered by all three monotheistic religions – Islam, Christianity, and Judaism. Over the period of many centuries, numerous wars have been fought and millions killed to claim rights over the city. Second, Jerusalem is one of the oldest cities in the world and its history spans a period of more than three thousand years. Finally, Jerusalem's history although different in Judeo-Christian and Islamic accounts, brings forth the many underlying differences that separate the beliefs of Islam, Christianity and Judaism.

All these factors make the task of writing this book very challenging. Such a rich history deserves many volumes, not merely a few pages of one book. However, the goal has been to provide the reader with an overview of the historical and religious reasons that make Jerusalem so revered by the followers of all three religions. Throughout the text the religious texts of all three religions (Quran, Bible, and Torah) are quoted to highlight the differences in beliefs because sometimes similar events transpired in history.

Most of the pre-historic accounts presented in the book are, therefore, based on the religious texts of the three religions. There are significantly wide differences in Judeo-Christian and Islamic versions. According to Islamic beliefs, one of the reasons why the message of Islam was brought to mankind was that the earlier nations had corrupted the divine message (and related stories in

Torah and Bible) and thus the need arose for the final and refreshed message in the Quran.

Readers should also take note that the message of Islam (revealed in 7th century CE on Prophet Muhammad) focused less on narrating the events of pre-historic times when Torah and Bible were revealed. The "Islamic version" of history from those times is, therefore, limited to what is mentioned in the Quran and related by Prophet Muhammad. Those accounts, especially those pertaining to Jerusalem, are presented in this book. Some of the history mentioned in this book from those times (pre-Islamic times) is also taken from Judeo-Christian books. An effort has been made to highlight the differences in the beliefs of such historical accounts wherever applicable.

The following example will be illustrative: Jewish scriptures extensively discuss "Temple Mount" in Jerusalem, a sacred site in Jewish history. However, Temple Mount has no direct mention in Islamic books of Quran and Hadith (saying and traditions of Prophet Muhammad). Similarly, the events leading to the crucifixion of Jesus in Jerusalem (as believed by Christians) are covered in more detail in Christian texts than the Islamic books, which provide a different version of those events.

Finally, the focus of this book has been to present facts from the different viewpoints rather than to provide an analysis of such events. Future versions of this e-book are expected to continue building on the work that has been covered to date. To stay updated on new releases of this book, please visit **www.IqraSense.com**.

2. Introduction

Jerusalem is known to be one of the oldest cities in the world and is the focal point of the three monotheist religions of the world— Judaism, Christianity and Islam. Each has a claim to the city of Jerusalem for reasons that are not fully understood by many. Today, more than ever, Jerusalem is at the center of a great political controversy that affects not only the Jewish people and the Muslims and Arabs in the region, but Christians as well, thus engulfing a major part of the globe. The sanctity of Jerusalem can be understood not just from the blood that has been shed in the modern conflict, but from the blood of the millions who have fought and been killed innocently in the thousands of years to date.

More than half of the world's population (approximately 55%[1]) consider Jerusalem sacred and revere it for various religious reasons. The city is highly revered by the followers of all Abrahamic religions namely Judaism, Christianity, and Islam. Jerusalem has a place in Judaism because of its beliefs rooted in the Biblical Zion, the City of David, and the city being the site of Solomon's Temple. Jerusalem holds the status of being the holiest city for Jews as they draw their spiritual links with the city since 1000 BCE, when David (known as Prophet Dawood in the Quran and Islamic texts) made it the first capital of Israel. According to the New Testament and the Gospels, Jesus (referred to as Prophet Eesa in Islamic texts) was brought to the city as a child and it was here that he preached and

---

[1] Major Religions of the World Ranked by Number of Adherents
http://www.adherents.com/Religions_By_Adherents.html

also healed. Christians also hold it high because it was where Jesus spent the last days of his ministry, and where the Last Supper, and according to Christian beliefs the Crucifixion and the Resurrection took place. Islam and Muslims honor Jerusalem because Jerusalem was Islam's first Qibla (direction for prayers) and it was from Jerusalem that Prophet Muhammad ascended to the heavens in the famous event that has come to be known as *"Al-Israa wal Me'raj"*. Muslims also revere Jerusalem as the third holiest site (according to religious teachings) behind the two cities **Makkah Al-Mukarramah** (known as Makkah) and **Madinah Al-Munawwara** (known as Madinah), both located in Saudi-Arabia. The Quran too includes many references to Jerusalem in a number of its verses to be explained later in this e-book.

The presence of historical landmarks of religious importance has also earned Jerusalem a position as a UNESCO World Heritage Site.2 The foundations of the city's oldest part, City of David, were laid in the 4th millennium BCE. Some of the key historical and religious sites in Jerusalem include the Haram al- Sharif, Al-Aqsa Mosque, Dome of the Rock, Church of the Holy Sepulcher, and the Western Wall.

---

[2] A UNESCO World Heritage Site is a place that is listed by the United Nations Educational, Scientific and Cultural Organization (UNESCO) as of special cultural or physical significance.

3. Prehistoric Jerusalem

a. The Name "Jerusalem"

Over the centuries, the followers of the Abrahamic religions have come to revere Jerusalem to such an extent that they have engaged in many conflicts claiming their rights over the city. The current day Jerusalem, therefore, continues to be disputed, particularly so amongst Jews and Muslims. According to Judeo-Christian historical accounts, during the biblical times, Jerusalem was the capital of the entire Kingdom of Israel (1020 BCE - 931 BC).[3] Later in history, Jerusalem became the capital of the Kingdom of Judah (930 BCE - 586 BC),[4] and consequently the chief city of Palestine.[5] Although Jerusalem witnessed numerous wars, the city was able to preserve

---

[3] Jerusalem was the capital of the Kingdom of Israel which was ruled by a united monarchy that lasted from 1020 BCE until its split in 930 BC. The kingdom had five kings, ruling one after the other: King Saul Shaul ben Qysh, 1030 BCE – 1010 BC); King Ishabaal (Ishba'al ben Shaul, 1010 BCE – 1008 BC), King David (David ben Yishai, 1008 BCE – 970 BC), King Solomon (Shelomon den David, 970 BCE – 931 BC), and Rehoboam (931 BCE – 930 BC). The territory of the Kingdom of Israel extended to the Phoenician States in the north (modern-day Lebanon), the Kingdoms of Aram-Damascus, Ammon and Moab to the west (modern day Damascus and Jordan, and the Kingdom of Judah to the south (modern day Saudi Arabia and Egypt).

[4] According to Judeo-Christian history, from the year 930 BCE to 586 BC, Jerusalem was made the capital of the Kingdom of Judah. The new Kingdom of Judah was originally part of the United Kingdom of Israel until 930 BCE when the Twelve Tribes of Israel rejected Solomon's son, Rehoboam, as their king. The new kingdom came to be known as the Southern Kingdom, while Israel was referred to as the Northern Kingdom. As a result of the split, half of the territorial land mass of Israel went to the new Kingdom of Judah.

[5] The term Palestine is the cognate (origin) of the word "*Philistines*" or "Land of the Philistines" which was used to refer to a group of people or tribe who occupied the southern coast of Canaan. The land was also referred to as Philistia, the modern-day Gaza. Today, the term Palestine is used broadly simply because Palestinians are still negotiating their rights to the land in and around Israel.

its name against the corrosive effects of history. The name Jerusalem ("Yerushalayim" in Hebrew) is known to have first appeared in old Hebrew coins during the Old Testament period. The name Yerushalayim has many variations in other languages, such as Aramaic (Yerushlem), Assyrian (Urusalim), Greek (Ιεροσόλυμα) and later Arabic (Urishalam). The root word, however, behind all the names was "Shalem" which means "peace".

b. The City of David

According to the Hebrew Bible, the Jebusites were a Canaanite[6] tribe who inhabited and built Jerusalem prior to its conquest by King David (b.1040 BC). The Books of Kings[7] state that Jerusalem was known as "Jebus" prior to this event. According to some Biblical chronologies, King David conquered the city in 1003 BCE and later, as King David ruled the city, the city significantly extended its territory as far as the southern hill or the Mount of Olives. The City of David is considered to be the oldest part of Jerusalem from which Jerusalem eventually flourished into a full-fledged city. Today, the City of David and its buildings are being preserved as a major archaeological site. David (who is referred to as Prophet Dawood in Islamic texts), ordered the construction of the palace, which came to

---

6 Canaan used to refer to a region that today encompasses Israel, Lebanon, parts of Jordan, Syria and parts of Egypt. The term is used in Hebrew Bible as well.

[7] The Books of Kings are books that are part of the Hebrew Bible. These books were originally written in Hebrew and are recognized as scripture by both Judaism and Christianity. The events stated in the Books of Kings occurred between the 10th and 6th centuries BC.

comprise of many buildings. The construction of the palace buildings took thirteen years to complete. It was, however, Solomon (referred to as Prophet Suleiman in Islamic texts), who significantly improved the city and its appearance. It was during Solomon's time that the wall surrounding the city was built. The construction of the temple too started during the time of Solomon and took seven years to complete. The temple, also referred to as "Solomon's temple", is regarded as sacred by the Jewish faith. The Temple was a place where most of the important Jewish festivities were commemorated, including the Feast of the Tabernacles.[8]

c. The Construction of the Temple

According to Jewish texts, the background and rationale behind the construction of the Temple was the realization of King David that he, the earthly and visible king, dwelled in a magnificent house, but the invisible king of kings, his God, dwelt in an aging tent called the Tabernacle of Moses.[9] Other than this humble realization, King David ultimately realized that other nations had temples of their own, while Israel, the chosen people of God, did not have a temple dedicated to Him.

---

[8] The Feast of the Tabernacles (also known as Sukkot or Feast of Booths) is a Jewish holiday celebrated on the 15th day of the month of Tishrei (late September to late October). It is the time when Jews made pilgrimages to the Temple in Jerusalem.

[9] According to the Hebrew Torah/Old Testament, Tabernacle of Moses was the portable sanctuary of the divine presence. As the people of Israel wandered through the land of Egypt and the Canaan, the Tabernacle of Moses was always with them as a sign that God was forever with them. It was eventually laid to rest in the First Temple of Jerusalem, which was constructed precisely to house it.

It was, therefore, David who commissioned the construction of the Temple, but it was his son Solomon who saw through the completion of the construction of the project. The role of David in the preparation of the details and plans for the Temple is recorded in Jewish texts (Chronicles 1: Chapter 22):

Therefore David said, "This is the house of the LORD God, and this is the altar of holocausts for Israel." David then ordered that all the aliens who lived in the land of Israel be brought together, and he appointed them stonecutters to hew out stone blocks for building the house of God. He also laid up large stores of iron to make nails for the doors of the gates, and clamps, together with so much bronze that it could not be weighed, and cedar trees without number. The Sidonians and Tyrians brought great stores of cedar logs to David, who said: "My son Solomon is young and immature; but the house that is to be built for the LORD must be made so magnificent that it will be renowned and glorious in all countries. Therefore I will make preparations for it." Thus before his death David laid up materials in abundance.

Then he called for his son Solomon and commanded him to build a house for the LORD, the God of Israel. David said to Solomon: "My son, it was my purpose to build a house myself for the honor of the LORD, my God. But this word of the LORD came to me: 'You have shed much blood, and you have waged great wars. You may not build a house in my honor, because you have shed too much blood upon the earth in my sight. However, a son is to be born to you. He will be a peaceful man, and I will give him rest from all his enemies on every side. For Solomon shall be his name, and in his time I will bestow peace and tranquility on Israel. It is he who shall build a house in my honor; he shall be a son to me, and I will be a father to him, and I will establish the throne of his kingship over Israel forever.' Now, my son, the LORD be with you, and may you succeed in building the house of the LORD your God, as he has said you shall.

May the LORD give you prudence and discernment when he brings you to rule over Israel, so that you keep the law of the LORD, your God. Only then shall you succeed, if you are careful to observe the precepts and decrees which the LORD gave Moses for Israel. Be brave and steadfast; do not fear or lose heart. See, with great effort I have laid up for the house of the LORD a hundred thousand talents of gold, a million talents of silver, and bronze and iron in such great quantities that they cannot be weighed. I have also stored up wood and stones, to which you must add. Moreover, you have available an unlimited supply of workmen, stonecutters, masons, carpenters, and every kind of craftsman skilled in gold, silver, bronze, and iron. Set to work, therefore, and the LORD be with you!"

David also commanded all of Israel's leaders to help his son Solomon: "Is not the LORD your God with you? Has he not given you rest on every side? Indeed, he has delivered the occupants of the land into my power, and the land is subdued before the LORD and his people. Therefore, devote your hearts and souls to seeking the LORD your God. Proceed to build the sanctuary of the LORD God, so that the ark of the covenant of the LORD and God's sacred vessels may be brought into the house built in honor of the LORD."

It should be noted again that these pre-historical facts are mostly based on Judeo-Christian texts. Islamic texts don't have any evidences about the sanctity or even existence of the temple, even though there are many references to Prophet Dawood (David) and Prophet Suleiman (Solomon) in the Quran and Hadith (Islamic texts). As will be mentioned later, Prophet Muhammad only referred to the building of the Al-Aqsa mosque at the site.

In general, the following are some of the verses from the Quran that refer to David, Solomon and other Abrahamic prophets:

"And indeed We gave knowledge to Dawud (David) and Suleiman (Solomon), and they both said: "All the praises and thanks be to Allah,[10] *Who has preferred us above many of His believing slaves!" (Quran 27:15)*

"Verily, We have sent the revelation to you (O Muhammad) as We sent the revelation to Nuh (Noah) and the Prophets after him; We (also) sent the revelation to Ibrahim (Abraham), Isma'il (Ishmael), Ishaq (Isaac), Ya'qub (Jacob), and Al-Asbat [the offspring of the twelve sons of Ya'qub (Jacob)], 'Îsa (Jesus), Ayyub (Job), Yunus (Jonah), Harun (Aaron), and Sulaiman (Solomon); and to Dawud (David) We gave the Zabur (Psalms)" (Quran 4: 163).

"And We bestowed upon him Ishaq (Isaac) and Ya'qub (Jacob), each of them We guided, and before him, We guided Nuh (Noah), and among his progeny Dawud (David), Sulaiman (Solomon), Ayyub (Job), Yusuf

---

[10] "Allah", according to Islam, is the one God that is the lord of the worlds. The Quran, which is the word of Allah revealed to Prophet Muhammad, describes Jews and Christians at great length. The word "Allah" in the Quran is used to refer to the God of Christians and Jews as well. In fact, Arab Christians and Arabic Bible refer to God as "Allah" as well. However, in general, western Christians for the most part recognize "Allah" as the God of Muslims only.

(Joseph), Musa (Moses), and Harun (Aaron). Thus do We reward Al-Muhsinun (the good-doers)" (Quran 6:84).

"And (remember) Dawud (David) and Sulaiman (Solomon), when they gave judgement in the case of the field in which the sheep of certain people had pastured at night; and We were witness to their judgement" (Quran 21:78).

"And to Dawud (David) We gave Sulaiman (Solomon). How excellent a slave! Verily, he was ever oft-returning in repentance (to Us)!" (Quran 38:30)

Upon David's death, his son King Solomon (b. 1011 BCE – d. 931 BC) ordered the construction of the Temple. Because of the enormity of the project, Solomon employed craftsmen from far flung areas to help build the Temple. The construction of the Temple began in the fourth year of Solomon's reign as King of Israel. King Solomon, who reigned from 970 BCE until 930 BC, completed the construction of the Temple in the year 957 BC. This temple is also commonly referred to as the **Temple of Solomon**.

The First Book of Kings (1 Kings 6), a Jewish religious book, provided the detailed description of the construction of the Temple under the guidance of Solomon. The following is an extract from that description:

In the four hundred and eightieth year from the departure of the Israelites from the land of Egypt, in the fourth year of Solomon's reign over Israel, in the month of Ziv, which is the second month, the construction of the temple of the LORD was begun.

The temple which King Solomon built for the LORD was sixty cubits long, twenty wide, and twenty-five high. The porch in front of the temple was twenty cubits from side to side, along the width of the nave, and ten cubits deep in front of the temple. Splayed windows with trellises were made for the temple, and adjoining the wall of the temple, which enclosed the nave and the sanctuary, an annex of several stories was built. Its lowest story was five cubits wide, the middle one six cubits wide, the third seven cubits wide, because there were offsets along the outside of the temple so that the beams would not be fastened into the walls of the temple. (The temple was built of stone dressed at the quarry, so that no hammer, axe, or iron tool was to be heard in the temple during its construction.) The entrance to the lowest floor of the annex was at the right side of the temple, and stairs with intermediate landings led up to the middle story and from the middle story to the third. When the temple was built to its full height, it was roofed in with rafters and boards of cedar. The annex, with its lowest story five cubits high, was built all along the outside of the temple, to which it was joined by cedar beams.

This word of the LORD came to Solomon: "As to this temple you are building—if you observe my statutes, carry out my ordinances, keep and obey all my commands, I will fulfill toward you the promise I made to your father David. I will dwell in the midst of the Israelites and will not forsake my people Israel."

When Solomon finished building the temple, its walls were lined from floor to ceiling beams with cedar paneling, and its floor was laid with fir planking. At the rear of the temple a space of twenty cubits was set off by cedar partitions from the floor to the rafters, enclosing the sanctuary, the holy of holies. The nave, or part of the temple in front of the sanctuary, was forty cubits long. The cedar in the interior of the temple was carved in the form of gourds and open flowers; all was of cedar, and no stone was to be seen.

In the innermost part of the temple was located the sanctuary to house the ark of the LORD'S covenant, twenty cubits long, twenty wide, and twenty high. Solomon overlaid the interior of the temple with pure gold. He made in front of the sanctuary a cedar altar, overlaid it with gold, and looped it with golden chains. The entire temple was overlaid with gold so that it was completely covered with it; the whole altar before the sanctuary was also overlaid with gold. In the sanctuary were two cherubim, each ten cubits high, made of olive wood. Each wing of a cherub measured five cubits so that the space from wing tip to wing tip of each was ten cubits. The cherubim were identical in size and shape, and each was exactly ten cubits high. The cherubim were placed in the inmost part of the temple, with their wings spread wide, so that one wing of each cherub touched a side wall while the other wing, pointing toward the middle of the room, touched the corresponding wing of the second cherub. The cherubim, too, were overlaid with gold.

The walls on all sides of both the inner and the outer rooms had carved figures of cherubim, palm trees, and open flowers. The floor of both the inner and the outer rooms was overlaid with gold. At the entrance of the sanctuary, doors of olive wood were made; the doorframes had beveled posts. The two doors were of olive wood, with carved figures of cherubim, palm trees, and open flowers. The doors were overlaid with gold, which was also molded to the cherubim and the palm trees. The same was done at the entrance to the nave, where the doorposts of olive wood were rectangular. The two doors were of fir wood; each door was banded by a metal strap, front and back, and had carved cherubim, palm trees, and open flowers, over which gold was evenly applied.

The inner court was walled off by means of three courses of hewn stones and one course of cedar beams.

The foundations of the LORD'S temple were laid in the month of Ziv in the fourth year, and it was completed in all particulars, exactly according to plan, in the month of Bul, the eighth month, in the eleventh year. Thus it took Solomon seven years to build it.

Later, in 586 BC, the Temple of Solomon (known also as the First Temple) along with other parts of the city of Jerusalem was destroyed by the Babylonians. Forty-eight years later in 538 BC, Cyrus the Great (b. 600 BCE – d. 530 BC), who was a Persian emperor, rebuilt the Second Temple. Centuries later, the same Temple underwent a massive reconstruction project under Herod the Great (b. 74 BCE – d. 1 BC) in the year 20 B.C, and became known as Herod's Temple. Finally, in the year 70 CE, the Romans destroyed the Second Temple during the great siege of Jerusalem.

d. Jerusalem at the Time of Jesus

Jesus of Nazareth, who is called by such names as Jesus Christ by Christians or Eesa in the Quran and other Islamic literature, was born in Bethlehem in the year 5 BC, but spent most of his life in

Jerusalem, the center of Judaism. According to Christian beliefs, Jesus eventually died of crucifixion in the year 30 CE between the age of 33 and 35 years. According to the Islamic belief, however, Jesus did not die of crucifixion. The Muslims believe, as mentioned in the Quran, that he was lifted to the heavens, and will return again to earth as a follower of Islam and Prophet Muhammad's teachings before his ultimate death.

The Gospel according to Matthew (1:18-25), a Christian text, provides an account of Jesus's birth near Jerusalem as follows:

Now this is how the birth of Jesus Christ came about. When his mother Mary was betrothed to Joseph, but before they lived together, she was found with child through the Holy Spirit. Joseph her husband, since he was a righteous man, yet unwilling to expose her to shame, decided to divorce her quietly. Such was his intention when, behold, the angel of the Lord appeared to him in a dream and said, "Joseph, son of David, do not be afraid to take Mary your wife into your home. For it is through the Holy Spirit that this child has been conceived in her. She will bear a son and you are to name him Jesus, because he will save his people from their sins." All this took place to fulfill what the Lord had said through the prophet:

"Behold, the virgin shall be with child and bear a son, and they shall name him Emmanuel," which means "God is with us."

When Joseph awoke, he did as the angel of the Lord had commanded him and took his wife into his home. He had no relations with her until she bore a son, and he named him Jesus.

The Quran too indirectly references Jerusalem and Bethlehem for the birth of Jesus. Although Jesus (Eesa) and Mary are mentioned in many parts of the Quran, the following are some of the verses related to Jesus's birth around Jerusalem.

And mention in the Book (the Quran, O Muhammad, the story of) Maryam (Mary), when she withdrew in seclusion from her family to a place facing east.

She placed a screen (to screen herself) from them; then We sent to her Our Ruh (angel Jibrael (Gabriel)), and he appeared before her in the form of a man in all respects.

She said: "Verily! I seek refuge with the Most Beneficent (Allah) from you, if you do fear Allah."

(The angel) said: "I am only a Messenger from your Lord, (to announce) to you the gift of a righteous son."

She said: "How can I have a son, when no man has touched me, nor am I unchaste?"

He said: "So (it will be), your Lord said: That is easy for Me (Allah): And (We wish) to appoint him as a sign to mankind and a mercy from Us (Allah), and it is a matter (already) decreed, (by Allah). "

So she conceived him, and she withdrew with him to a far place (i.e. Bethlehem valley about 4-6 miles from Jerusalem).

And the pains of childbirth drove her to the trunk of a date-palm. She said: "Would that I had died before this, and had been forgotten and out of sight!"

Quran (19: 16-23)

The details of the Islamic beliefs about Jesus are out of the scope of this book.

Ibn Kathir,[11] an Islamic scholar and one of the most notable Quran interpreters provides the following explanation:

> *"The scholars differed over its location. As-Suddi said, "Her place of seclusion was to the east and that was where she would pray at the Sacred House of Jerusalem." Wahb bin Munabbih said, "She ran away and when she reached an area between Ash-Sham and Egypt, she was overcome by labor pains." In another narration from Wahb, he said, "This took place eight miles from the Sacred House of Jerusalem in a village that was known as Bayt Al-Lahm (Bethlehem)." I say, there are Hadiths about the Isra' (Night Journey of the Prophet) that are reported by An-Nasa'i on the authority of Anas, and Al-Bayhaqi on the authority of Shadad bin Aws, that say that this took place at Bait Al-Lahm (Bethlehem). Allah knows best. This is what is well known that the people all relate from each other. The Christians have no doubt held that the place of this occurrence was Bethlehem and this is what all the people relate."*

As Jesus (Eesa) reached adulthood, he spent most of his time in Jerusalem. Jerusalem at that time was "a small, isolated hill fortress, valued more for its location than its size or splendor."[12] At that time, however, Jerusalem was known as the City of David.

---

[11] Ibn Kathir (1301–1373 CE) wrote one of the most followed famous commentaries on the Quran named "Tafsir al-Quran al-'Adhim". In this commentary he linked certain Hadith (Prophet Muhammad's sayings), and sayings of the sahaba (prophet's companions) to verses of the Quran. Tafsir Ibn Kathir is famous throughout the Muslim world and is considered as one of the most authentic and widely used explanations of the Quran today.

[12] See "Jerusalem at the Time of Christ." Bible History.

Jerusalem, at the time of Jesus (Eesa), was already the center of commerce. There were open-air shops where many of the craftsmen worked. These included dyers, weavers, bakers, potters, carpenters, tailors and metalworkers. In other areas of Jerusalem, there were merchants who sold various items like jewelry, perfumes, clothes, sacrificial animals, vegetables and dried fish. As always, the market area was crowded and busy during market days when citizens and visitors would come to Jerusalem to buy goods. During the Sabbath,[13] the market was closed.

During the time of Jesus (Eesa), Jerusalem's working class lived in the crowded and noisy precincts of lower Jerusalem. Their one or two storey ordinarily looking houses were a reflection of their lifestyles. The rich and powerful Jewish families, on the other hand, along with the high ranking Roman officials, lived in upper Jerusalem in elegantly fashioned houses patterned after the architecture in Rome and Greece.

Although Jesus (Eesa) was born in Bethlehem, as also narrated in the Biblical texts of the Gospel of Matthew, the significance of Jerusalem to the life of Jesus (Eesa) is rather deep. It was in Jerusalem where Jesus spent the last months of his life on this earth where he was sentenced to death and was crucified (per Christian beliefs) in Golgotha, a place located just outside the wall of Jerusalem. The Gospel of Matthew, a Christian text, narrates the final moments of Jesus in Jerusalem (Matthew 27:33-44) as follows:

---

[13] The Sabbath (*Shabbath*) is a weekly rest observed by the Jews from sundown on Friday until Saturday night.

And when they came to a place called Golgotha (which means Place of the Skull), they gave Jesus wine to drink mixed with gall. But when he had tasted it, he refused to drink. After they had crucified him, they divided his garments by casting lots; then they sat down and kept watch over him there. And they placed over his head the written charge against him: This is Jesus, the King of the Jews. Two revolutionaries were crucified with him, one on his right and the other on his left. Those passing by reviled him, shaking their heads and saying, "You who would destroy the temple and rebuild it in three days, save yourself, if you are the Son of God, (and) come down from the cross!" Likewise the chief priests with the scribes and elders mocked him and said, "He saved others; he cannot save himself. So he is the king of Israel! Let him come down from the cross now, and we will believe in him. He trusted in God; let him deliver him now if he wants him. For he said, 'I am the Son of God.'" The revolutionaries who were crucified with him also kept abusing him in the same way.

e. *Jerusalem before the "fall"*

Before the collapse of Jerusalem at the hands of the Romans in the year 70 CE (many years after Jesus's crucifixion event), a diverse group of people inhabited the city. This included the Jewish majority, the Zealots, and the Hellenists or Greeks.[14] As the city of Jerusalem

---

[14] The Zealots (zealot, which means on behalf of God) were members of a political movement or sect during the first century Judaism. They were active in inciting the Jewish people to rebel against the Romans, who were occupying Jerusalem at that time. The Hellenists were the Greeks who were residing in Jerusalem (*Hellen*, means Greek).

at this time came under the Roman Empire, many Romans also lived in the city. During Jewish festivities, Jews would come to the city from the farthest portions of the Diaspora[15] to celebrate their feasts, including the Feast of the Passover. In the accounts of historian Tacitus, the city of Jerusalem at that time was the face of modernity. There were high walls with towers as high as 120 feet and the city had a large fountain of water. No one knew at the time that Jerusalem's grandeur was soon to collapse.

f. The Destruction of Jerusalem (70 CE)

In the year 70 CE, Jerusalem witnessed the most destructive effects of war from the population that dwelled within the city. The primary cause of the collapse of Jerusalem was the disagreement and dissention of its own population who were composed of diverse cultures and beliefs. Another factor was the greed of the Roman procurators,[16] particularly **Gessius Florus** (procurator, 64 CE – 66 CE) who was known for his harsh behavior toward Jerusalem's Jewish people. Later, **Cestius Gallus** took over from Florus, who vanished into Caesarea (a town in Israel), and tried to recover his fortune. The reign of Gallus saw another wrath in Jerusalem. He was responsible for conquering and burning the new city of Beit

---

[15] The Jewish diaspora (or simply the Diaspora), is the English term used to describe the Jews in exile.

[16] The Roman procurators were government financial agents in ancient Rome. They were responsible for supervising the imperial finances in their respective jurisdictions, in this case Jerusalem.

She'arim (also called Bezetha), but he failed to take control of the Temple Mount (site of Al-Aqsa in Jerusalem).

However, it was during the rule of Roman Emperor *Titus Flavius Vespasianus* (Vespasian, b. 9 CE – d. 79 CE) that the great siege of Jerusalem took place that lasted from the 14th of Nisan[17] until the 8th of Elul[18] or for about 134 days. When the son of Vespasian, Titus Flavius Vespasianus (Titus, b. 39 CE – d. 81 CE), took over the reins of power, the wall of Agrippa (the most northerly wall that enclosed the city) was captured on the fifteenth day of the siege; on the twentieth and the twenty-fourth, the second wall of Jerusalem was taken; on the twenty-second, the Antonia Fortress, which was a military barracks close to the second wall of Jerusalem, was taken; and on the eighty-fourth day of the siege, the Temple sacrifices[19] and related worships were totally stopped. The destruction of Jerusalem continued, and on the ninety-fifth day, the northern cloisters of the Temple were destroyed; on the one hundred and fifth day, fire was set to the Temple, resulting in the burning of the lower city, and then finally the rest of the city of Jerusalem was burned.

According to Judeo-Christian prehistoric accounts, the destruction of Jerusalem was so vast that even the walls of the city were leveled and the inhabitants were sold as slaves in the Roman markets. Later, Hadrian (Publius Aelius Hadrianus, b. 76 CE – d. 138 CE),

---

[17] Nisan is the seventh month of the year in the Hebrew calendar having 30 days. It corresponds to March / April in the Gregorian calendar.

[18] Elul is the 12th month of the year in the Hebrew calendar with 29 days. It corresponds to August / September in the Gregorian calendar.

[19] Although no animal sacrifices are held at the temple location because there is no temple in the current day Jerusalem, a few extremist Jews have been attempting to start the practice in recent times by approaching the Al-Aqsa compound, also referred to as Temple Mount by Jews.

who reigned from 117 A.D. until his death in 138 CE, attempted to build a Roman city on the ruins of Jerusalem and to convert the city into a pagan worshipping capital. He also dedicated the temple to various pagan gods and made sanctuaries for Jupiter and Venus in the Temple in an attempt to dislocate the Jews. The statutes of Emperor Hadrian were then built and placed alongside that of Jupiter, the Roman god of love, in the Temple area.

4. Jerusalem under the Islamic Rule

When the Roman Empire, to which Jerusalem belonged, came under the rule of Emperor Constantine I (b. 272 CE – d. 337 CE), Jerusalem started to turn more "Christian". Churches started to sprout in Jerusalem to give credence to the life of Jesus who once walked through Jerusalem. For a long time after that Jerusalem was under the influence of the Christian emperors until the city was conquered by the Arabs. The Islamic rule began with the conquest of Jerusalem by **Umar Khattab's** forces. Later, under the rule of Umayyad Caliph Abd al-Malik ibn Marwan (b. 646 CE – d. 705 CE), the Dome of the Rock was built in 688 CE followed by the copula of the Al-Aqsa Mosque in the year 728 CE. The Dome of the Rock underwent a series of renovations in 831 CE and it was also during this time that the octagonal wall was erected. In an earthquake in 1016 CE, the Dome of the Rock was partly damaged, but it was immediately repaired in 1022 CE.

According to Islamic beliefs, Al-Aqsa mosque was built very early in history. Although Al-Aqsa mosque located in Jerusalem is considered as Islam's third holiest site (after Makkah and Madinah), Al-Aqsa mosque was the second house established on earth for the worship of One God. According to a Hadith (saying) of Prophet Muhammad as quoted by Abu Dharr (Narrated in the books by al-Bukhaari, 3186 and Muslim, 520):

> *"O Messenger of Allah, which mosque was built first on earth?" He said, "Al-Masjid al-Haraam (in Makkah)." I said, "Then which?" He said, "Al-Masjid al-Aqsa. (in*

Jerusalem)" I asked, "How much time was between them?" He said, "Forty years. So wherever you are when the time for prayer comes, then pray."

After the Crusades during the 11th century, the city of Jerusalem was captured by the Egyptian Mamluks in the middle of the 13th century. But in the year 1517 CE, Jerusalem was back under Islamic rule under the powerful hand of the Ottoman Empire that ruled the city until the empire's decline in the middle of 19th century when the British came out victorious over the Ottoman Turks in World War I. This was the beginning of the British rule in Jerusalem known in history as the British Mandate of Palestine. The British rule in Jerusalem lasted until 1948 when the city suffered the most devastating effects of war. Jerusalem, for the first time in history, was divided into two: the western half went to the newly created Jewish state of Israel while the eastern half was annexed to Muslim Jordan.

The period from the first Islamic rule until today is covered in the next few sections of this book.

a. Conquest by Caliph Umar (638 AD)

After the death of Prophet Muhammad, Umar ibn al-Khattab's forces conquered Jerusalem.[20] During Umar's reign, Jerusalem was

---

[20] Umar was the second Islamic Caliph after Abu-Bakr al-Siddiq. Abu-Bakr was the first Muslim Caliph (ruler) appointed after the death of Prophet Muhammad.

conquered bloodlessly for the first time by Muslims in the year 638 CE. As Muhammad had laid the foundation of the religion of Islam (through revelation from God, Allah), Umar's conquest of Jerusalem is considered to be the first in Islamic history.

During Umar's reign, Muslims won many battles, most notable of which was the battle of Yarmouk. The battle was fought between Umar's forces and the armies of the East Roman-Byzantine Empire. The battle lasted for six days in August 636 CE, near the Yarmouk River, along what is today the border between Syria and Jordan, south-east of the Sea of Galilee. The Battle of Yarmouk is regarded as one of the most decisive battles in military history and marked the first wave of Islamic conquests after the death of Muhammad, heralding the rapid advance of Islam into the then Christian Levant.[21] This battle permanently ended the Byzantine rule south of Anatolia (western part of Asia mostly consisting of Turkey and also referred to as "Asia Minor").

During these conquests, as the Muslim forces marched toward Jerusalem, the Byzantines were forced to leave Syria. The Muslim armies under the commandership of *Amr ibn Al-As* reached Jerusalem and lay siege of the city. Amr was later joined by prominent Muslim commanders such as *Khalid bin Waleed* and *Abu Ubaidah ibn al Jarrah*. At that time, *Bishop Sophronius* was the Patriarch[22] of Jerusalem. Sophronius, who was of an Arab

---

[21] The Levant includes Lebanon, Syria, Jordan, and Iraq. Occasionally Cyprus, Sinai, and Israel are also included. The UCL Institute of Archeology describes the Levant as the "crossroads of western Asia, the eastern Mediterranean and northeast Africa."

[22] In general, the highest-ranking bishops in Eastern Orthodoxy, and the Roman Catholic Church, are called patriarchs.

descent, is venerated as a saint in the Catholic as well as the Eastern Orthodox Church. Seeing little hope in resisting, the Christians in Jerusalem decided to surrender at the hands of Caliph Umar's forces. However, the Bishop demanded that the city keys would be handed over to the Muslims without resistance only if Caliph Umar personally received the city keys. Muslims at that time didn't favor entertaining the patriarch's demands saying that as the Christian forces had been vanquished, they were in no position to dictate terms and thus there was no need for the Caliph to go to Jerusalem. Caliph Umar sought the advice of Ali,[23] one of the Prophet's closet aides. Ali instead advised Umar to go to Jerusalem on the ground that he was the victor and that it was from Jerusalem that the Holy Prophet ascended the Heavens. On this, Caliph Umar agreed to go to Jerusalem to accept the Christian surrender. When Umar entered the city, he first asked about the location of the site of Al-Aqsa and the Rock from where Muhammad ascended for Me'raj. At that time, the Dome of the Rock had not yet been built. The Bishop took him to the site (known to the Jews as Temple Mount), which to Umar's disappointment was being used as a garbage dump. This is because under the Christian rule at that time, Jews were not allowed to worship or even enter Jerusalem and the Al-Aqsa site (Temple Mount) had no specific religious significance for the Christians. He also found out that the Al-Aqsa mosque was destroyed by the Romans. On seeing the state of the Al-Aqsa site (Temple Mount), Umar said:

---

[23] Ali became the Caliph after the reign of Uthman, who in turn became the Caliph after the assassination of Umar.

"Allah (God) is Great, I swear by the one who holds my soul in his hand that this is the Mosque of David which the prophet of Allah described to us after his night journey." [24]

The Caliph then asked **Kaab al-Ahbar,** a Jewish Rabbi who had converted to Islam and came with Umar from Medina, to guide him to the place of the Rock. Umar used his clothes to remove the trash covering the Rock, and other Muslims followed Umar and they cleaned the Al-Aqsa site. Umar also fenced the rock and an Umayyad ruler later built the Dome of the Rock on the Al-Aqsa site (the site on which stand the Dome of the Rock and the Al-Aqsa Mosque.)

In Jerusalem, Caliph Umar was also taken to the Church of Holy Sepulcher and was offered the opportunity by the Christian leadership to pray in the church. The Caliph, in the view of Muslims, acted with prudence and refused to pray inside the church. He feared that future Muslim generations might decide to follow his footsteps and demand that the church be converted into a mosque. The Caliph therefore preferred to pray outside and a mosque was later built in his name called the **Mosque of Umar**. This mosque is currently located opposite the southern courtyard of the church.

On the surrender of Jerusalem's Patriarch Sophronius, no killing or destruction was carried out by Muslims. It was a peaceful transition and all the holy sites of Christians were left untouched. Caliph Umar

---

[24] Al-Aqsa Mosque - http://muslimwiki.com/mw/index.php/Al-Aqsa_Mosque

signed a treaty with Sophronius and as a result, Christians were allowed to live in the city. The treaty Umar signed was as follows:

> *From the servant of Allah and the Commander of the Faithful, Omar: The inhabitants of Jerusalem are granted security of life and property. Their churches and crosses shall be secure. This treaty applies to all people of the city. Their places of worship shall remain intact. These shall neither be taken over nor pulled down. People shall be quite free to follow their religion. They shall not be put to any trouble...[25]*

History notes that before the Muslim conquest of Jerusalem, the Jews were not allowed to live inside the city. Although Jews were eventually allowed to come to Jerusalem for worship, the Christian ruler had requested that the Jews were not to be allowed to live in Jerusalem. Under the surrender terms, Caliph Umar accepted that request. However, later the Muslims relaxed the rules and the Jews were also allowed to enter the city and settle with the rest of the population. Caliph Umar also assured the Christian ruler that the Christians would have full rights under the Muslim rule and they would not be harmed in any way. They would have complete protection as specifically directed by Islamic laws. The Muslim rulers following Caliph Umar understood the nobility of Jerusalem in the hearts of Jews and Christians and thus the three religions started to practice their beliefs freely in Jerusalem.

---

[25] New World Encyclopedia - http://www.newworldencyclopedia.org/entry/Umar_ibn_al-Khattab

In course of time, many scholars belonging to the three religions came and settled in Jerusalem. For Muslims, Jerusalem, especially the Al-Aqsa mosque, became a large hub of learning. It also became common for Muslims to start mentioning in their wills the desire to be buried in Jerusalem. This is one of the reasons why there are thousands of Muslim graves in Jerusalem. The Muslim rulers later also built many schools, religious centers and hospitals in Jerusalem. Large areas of land was purchased and dedicated to religious activities.

b. Umayyad Caliphate (661 – 750 AD)

After the death of **Ali bin Abi Talib**, who was the fourth and the last of the prominent Rashidun caliphs, the Umayyad Caliphate started to take root as the rulers of the newly established Islamic empire. The Umayyads were from Makkah and the dynasty drew its name from **Umayya ibn Abd Shams** who was the great grandfather of the first Umayyad dynasty caliph. Once in power, they chose Damascus as the capital of their empire, which is known to be one of the largest empires that existed in history.

The first caliph of the Umayyad rule was **Amir Muawiyah** who reigned from 661 to 680 CE. He was followed by his son Yazid who ruled from 680 to 683 CE. Under the rule of the Umayyads, Jerusalem was part of the province called **"Jund Filastin"** and included areas that are in the present day Palestinian territories. This province was part of the greater province of Syria. The original local capital of Filastin was the city of Ludd and was later changed to Ramla. After the Fatimids conquered the district from the Abbasids (the ruling dynasty after the Umayyads), Jerusalem eventually became the capital of Filastin.

With Umayyads' caliphate seat near Damascus, the proximity to the city of Jerusalem allowed them to pay special attention to the city and its development. When the Muslims had captured the city under Caliph Umar's reign, the city was more Christian in character and gave a look of a true Byzantine-Christian city. The Umayyads worked to change that look and thus most of their developments were to transform Jerusalem's look to being a Muslim city. In pursuance of this aim, they built the Al-Aqsa mosque and the Dome of the Rock at the Al-Aqsa site. They also restored the walls of the Haram al-Sharif (Al-Aqsa mosque). In the 1970s, six massive structures were uncovered during the excavations. Common speculation is that these buildings were the administrative center of the Umayyads. The Umayyads had also carried out enormous constructions on the south slope of Haram al- Sharif. These buildings were separated by paved streets. The builders also inserted clay pipes in the stones of the wall of Haram al- Sharif. This allowed running water to be provided from the main aqueduct. Large cisterns were also made beneath the buildings where rain water was collected. Extensive and elaborate drainage system was also installed. The Umayyads also built a series of buildings and palaces toward the south of Haram al- Sharif and these structures covered a vast area.

Today, the Dome of the Rock stands as the second most important Muslim building in Jerusalem (after the Al-Aqsa mosque). The building was completed in 691-692 CE. According to Muslim religious beliefs, this building houses the rock from where Prophet Muhammad went for Me'raj (ascension to the heavens). Muslims believe that the Prophet stepped on this stone and then ascended to the skies. In 701 CE, it was the Caliph al-Walid I who had the Al-Aqsa mosque rebuilt.

The administrative centers of the Umayyads included other buildings and palaces. They built typical palaces with numerous rooms and a courtyard in the center. The most impressive palace was built near the Haram al- Sharif's southwest corner. This palace was built as a seat for the Caliph when he visited Jerusalem. It also happens to be the largest palace in Jerusalem. A bridge was also constructed from this palace to the Al-Aqsa mosque.

c. Abbasid Caliphate (750 – 969 CE)

The Umayyad dynasty ruled for many years. In the later years, due to infighting and turmoil, the reign of the Muslim empire was taken over by the Abbasids who overthrew the Umayyad dynasty in 750 CE. The Abbasid family of caliphs was related to **Abbas ibn Abd al-Muttalib** who was Prophet Muhammad's uncle. The direct relation with the Prophet led the Abbasids to believe that they had more right over the caliphate than any other family. During the last years of the Umayyad rule, Abbasids started criticizing the Umayyad administration and more importantly the Umayyad rulers' moral character, and started to rebel against the Umayyad rule. In 750 CE, the Abbasids overthrew the Umayyad regime and killed a number of them on the grounds of corruption.

After taking over the rule, the Abbasids moved their capital from Damascus to Baghdad. The era of the Abbasid Caliphs (which was the third caliphate after the Rashidun and Umayyad caliphate) in the middle of 8th century, is known as the Islamic Golden Age. Abbasids stayed in power in varying capacities (political and sometimes religious) for more than seven centuries until their role ended with the transfer of power in 1519 CE. Their rule was briefly disrupted when *Halagu Khan* attacked Baghdad in 1258 CE. During the Abbasids' time, Baghdad became the new centre of learning and culture for the whole world. The Abbasids established a House of Wisdom in Baghdad where they employed non-Muslim and Muslim scholars to gather knowledge from all around the world and translate it into Arabic. Baghdad became the unrivalled champion in philosophy, science, education and medicine. Knowledge was gained and centralized about ancient civilizations like Chinese, Roman, Indian, Egyptian, Greek, Byzantine and North African, thus opening channels for people of diverse backgrounds who started coming to Baghdad to seek knowledge of various disciplines.

The holy shrines and sanctuaries of Jerusalem were renovated time and again by the Abbasid Caliphs of Baghdad. Other port cities under the Islamic rule like Acre, Arsuf, Jaffa, Haifa, Caesarea and Ashkelon received money from the state's treasury and were also made stronger by fortifying them.

Every year merchants from different cities would come to Jerusalem to take part in various trade fairs. Jerusalem became a major trading hub for goods such as spices, olive oils, soaps, glassware, silks and various European products. Christians continued to actively make pilgrimage to Jerusalem and Christian holy places in Jerusalem continued to get generous donations made by European Christian pilgrims. It was also during the Abbasid caliphate (specifically during Harun Rashid's time) that the first contact with the Frankish Kingdom of **Charlemagne** took place. This contact held great importance because it resulted in the construction of many churches in Jerusalem from the money sent by Charlemagne.

Although the Abbasids were less frequent visitors of Jerusalem than the Ummayads, they still carried on the modernization and construction in Jerusalem. For example, in 758 CE, **Al-Mansur** ordered the Dome of the Rock to be renovated which had collapsed as a result of an earthquake.

The Abbasids, however, didn't tend to other affairs of Palestine as much as the Umayyads. One of the reasons was that the Abbasids had moved their caliphate from Damascus (closer to Jerusalem) to Baghdad. In those areas various Arab tribes had formed local federations. Disputes amongst those tribes led to many battles between these Arab tribes in the period 793 – 796 CE during which many were killed. The ongoing civil war thus resulted in a major destruction of Palestinian areas.

During the reign of the Abbasids, the Muslim world saw the height of its power and glory. However, around 842 CE, during the caliphate of **al-Wathiq**, the power of the caliphate started to decline. The region around Iraq fell to the Buyid Dynasty, by 945 CE. Although the Abbasids remained caliphs, their role was diminished to being only ceremonial in nature.

Other dynasties also ruled other parts of the Muslim world during these periods. The Zengid (or Zangid) dynasty was one that ruled parts of Syria and northern Iraq on behalf of the Seljuk Empire. The Seljuq Empire controlled a vast area that stretched from the Hindu Kush to eastern Anatolia and also included regions in Central Asia and the Persian Gulf. They ruled those areas from 1037 CE to 1194 CE. The Ayyubid dynasty, on the other hand, was a Sunni Muslim dynasty of Kurdish origin centered in Cairo and Damascus that ruled much of the Middle East during the 12th and 13th centuries CE. The Ayyubid dynasty (to which Salah-ud-Din, son of Ayyub, belonged) ruled parts of the Muslim world from 1171 CE to 1341 CE.

d. Mamluk Rule (1270–1516 CE)

Under the rule of Ṣalah-ad-Din (covered later) and the Ayyubid dynasty of Egypt, the Mamluks became powerful until they claimed the rule in 1250, ruling as the Mamluk Sultanate. By the time of the fall of the Ayyubids, most Mamluks were Kipchak Turks.[26] The term "Mamluk" literally means "owned" in Arabic. Mamluks were soldiers of slave origin who had converted to Islam and lived during the period 9th to the 19th century CE. Later, Mamluks became a powerful

---

[26] Kipchaks were an ancient Turkic people. The term Turkic represents a broad ethno-linguistic group of people including existing societies such as the Kazakhs, Tatars, Kyrgyzs, Turkish, Turkmen, Uyghur, Uzbeks, as well as past civilizations such as the Seljuks, Khazars, Ottomans, Mamluks, Timurids, and others. (Wikipedia)

military and political force in various Muslim societies, especially in the areas of Egypt, the Levant, Iraq, and India. In some cases, they became the ruling class, while in others they held regional power as local governors. Some Mamluk factions seized the ruling power themselves in Egypt and Syria in a period known as the Mamluk Sultanate that lasted from 1250 CE to 1517 CE. Most notably, during the Mamluk rule, they defeated the Mongols and fought the Crusaders.

Starting in 1486 CE, hostilities broke out between the Mamluks and the Ottoman Turks in a battle for control over western Asia. The Mamluk armies were eventually defeated by the forces of the Ottoman Sultan, **Selim I**, and lost control of Palestine after the 1516 battle of **Marj Dabiq.**

e. The Period of the Ottoman Empire (1516 - 1917 CE)

The Ottoman Empire took power around 1299 CE and ruled until their defeat at the hands of the British during World War I in 1923 CE. They were at the height of their power in 16th and 17th centuries and controlled much of Southeastern Europe, Western Asia and North Africa. Countries would become part of the empire by taking an allegiance to the ruling Sultan or Caliph. Due to their control of Europe and Asia, the empire served to connect Europe and Asia. It can easily be said that Ottoman Empire was one of the biggest empires following the Roman Empire many centuries before the Ottomans.

Following the defeat of the Mamluk rule, the Ottomans ruled over Jerusalem until their defeat during World War I. As was the case under previous Islamic rulers, people of all faiths namely Muslims, Jews, Orthodox, Catholics, Assyrians, Coptic Christians, Protestants, Latins, etc., were able to live and practise their religion in Jerusalem.

The Ottomans continued to renovate the Islamic sites in Jerusalem during their rule. For example, they renovated the Dome of the Rock with calligraphic and nicer looking tiles, which can be found even today. The Ottoman ruler also had the distinction of being the custodian of Islam's all three holy sites, namely Makkah, Madinah, and Jerusalem. Under the rule of Sultan Suleiman (known to some as Suleiman the Magnificent), Jerusalem's walls were restored and permanent water supply was brought to the city. Suleiman, therefore, attempted to build the infrastructure of Jerusalem the signs of which are still visible in the city.

5. The Crusades – Wars for Jerusalem and the "Holy Lands"

The primary objective of the series of Crusades that were launched on Jerusalem and lasted for nearly two hundred years was to recover the Holy Land from the growing influence of Islam. The Crusades were thus Holy wars fought between the Muslims and the Christians, to gain control of Jerusalem and the surrounding areas. The principal proponent of the Crusades was the Latin Christian Europe, particularly the Holy Roman Empire and the Franks of France. For the Latin Christian Europe, the Holy Land held a significant role because it is the locus of the birth, ministry, believed crucifixion and resurrection of Jesus of Nazareth.

The term "crusade" is actually a broad concept of war that is applied, not only against the Muslims, but to all wars undertaken in pursuance of a vow. There were crusades against the Moors, Prussians, Lithuanians and the Albigensian heretics. However, the period between 1095 and 1291 CE was the time when the Crusades specifically directed to restore Christian control of the Holy Land from the Muslims. One unique factor of these Crusades was the solemn vow that was taken from the pope to deliver the Holy Land from the hands of the Muslims. As a result, the Crusaders were granted penance (forgiveness) of past sins by the pope. The wars were, therefore, religiously sanctioned for the Christians by the church and by the pope, to be more precise.

a. The First Crusade (1095-1099)

The preparations of the first Crusade started in March 1095 at the Council of Piacenza when Byzantine **Emperor Alexius I** (Alexios I Komnenos, b. 1056 – d. 1118) sent representatives to seek help to defend his empire from the Seljuk Turks, who were Turco-Persian Sunni Muslims that ruled the Middle East and some parts of Central Asia from the 11th to 14th centuries.

To provide some background, by the year 1055 the Seljuk Turk forces led by **Tughrul** had taken over Baghdad. The Seljuks not only consolidated and gave strength to the empire but also made new conquests and expanded their control up to Anatolia. In 1071, the Byzantine Emperor was defeated by the Turks in the Battle of Manzikert. This brought the whole of Asia Minor, modern Turkey, under the control of Turks. This was a grave situation for Emperor Alexius as it had weakened his position amongst his people and allies.

Emperor Alexius I thus called upon Pope Urban II (Otho de Lagery, b. 1088 – d. 1099), to help him against the invading Seljuk Turks. As a result, the Pope called all Christians to unite against the Muslims in an effort to stop their conquests and to recapture the Holy land. The Pope called upon the Christians to take a solemn vow to wage war against the Muslim Seljuk Turks with a promise that anyone who died would receive immediate remission of sins. Many Christians responded to the call and by August 1096, the crusader armies from France and Italy journeyed eastward toward Constantinople. The goals of the crusade were thus the Christian conquest of the sacred city of Jerusalem and the Holy Land and freeing the Eastern Christians from more than four centuries of Islamic rule.

When the Crusaders reached the city, they captured Jerusalem. This capture was marked by extensive destruction and killings in and around the city. The eyewitness accounts from the crusaders themselves leave little doubt that there was great slaughter in the aftermath of the siege.[27] During the assault, **Tancred** was one of the first Crusaders to enter the city. When the city fell, Tancred gave his banner to a group of citizens who had fled from the killings to the roof of the top of Al-Aqsa mosque in an assurance that they would be granted a safe passage from the killings. However, history notes that the promises were not kept and they were massacred by the Crusaders. Many in history dispute that the killings happened without the knowledge and approval of Tancred. The author of the **Gesta Francorum** (Deeds of the Franks) records that, when Tancred realized this, he was "greatly angered" by the massacre that was carried out by the Crusaders in Al-Aqsa mosque. Later, when the Kingdom of Jerusalem was established, Tancred became the Prince of Galilee.

As the assault continued, countless Jews were burned alive in their main synagogue where they had huddled together for refuge. Al-Aqsa and the Dome of the Rock were desecrated and looted. A golden cross was placed on top of the Dome of the Rock and renamed as *"Templum Domini"* (The Temple of the Lord) and Al Aqsa mosque was called *"Templum Salomonis"* (the royal palace

---

[27] First Crusade – http://en.wikipedia.org/wiki/First_Crusade

of Solomon).[28] Later, the whole city went through a complete demographic change to give it a "Christian" look. After destroying mosques and buildings of other religions, the crusaders concentrated on building churches, pilgrim hostels, monasteries, etc. Most of the buildings built were the ones which were to be used for religious purposes.

After the conquest of the first Crusade, the Christian Crusaders established four Crusader states under the Holy Roman Empire. They were as follows:

1. **Kingdom of Jerusalem** – Initially, it was a collection of small towns but later it expanded to include areas that include modern-day Israel, Lebanon, and the Palestinian territories.
2. **County of Edessa** – County of Edessa was based around the city of Edessa located in town in northern Mesopotamia.
3. **Principality of Antioch** – The Principality of Antioch included cities that are in modern day Turkey and Syria.
4. **County of Tripoli** – County of Tripoli was in the area of modern day Lebanon, around the city of modern Tripoli.

The above details demonstrate that the Crusaders were able to capture a large area in their first Crusade against the Muslims.

---

[28] The Temple Mount in Jerusalem –
http://www.templemount.org/history.htm

b. Knight Templars

Knight Templars were one of the most famous Western Christian military orders that were endorsed by the Catholic Church in 1129 CE. Within the Christian rule, they were considered as the most skilled fighting units of the Crusades and existed for a period of about two centuries. The Templars were initially created to protect the Christian pilgrims visiting Jerusalem and the Holy Lands. **King Baldwin II** of Jerusalem gave the Templars space for headquarters in the captured Al Aqsa Mosque ("Templum Salomonis"). Although the Templar military order started with few financial resources, they grew to become quite resourceful and powerful in a short period. Their status, however, was closely tied to the Crusades. When the Crusades' support faded in the mid 12th century after their defeat at the hands of Muslim rulers such as Salahuddin, the Templars' influence started to fade. In 1317 CE, the Knight Templars were officially disbanded.

c. The Second Crusade (1147-1149)

The Crusaders' dominance over Jerusalem (gained during the First Crusade) was short-lived because Muslims reunited again under the guidance of Turkish leader Imad al-Din Zengi (b. 1085 - d. 1146), who was the prince of the Zengid Dynasty. Muslims under Zengi not only recaptured Jerusalem from the Crusaders but expanded their control to more adjoining areas as well. When the Muslims led by Zengi captured the County of Edessa (formed during the first crusade) in 1144 CE, Europe witnessed a growing uproar to launch yet another crusade to recover the lost Holy Lands from the Muslims. The Second Crusade was then announced by **Pope Eugene III**.

The Pope called upon **Bernard of Clairvaux** (b. 1090 – d. 1153), a Frankish abbot, to preach the Second Crusade and granted the same indulgences for it which Pope Urban II had accorded to the First Crusade. Bernard, therefore, called upon all Christians to join the Crusade. King Louis VII (b. 1120 – d. 1180) of France and King Conrad III (b. 1093 – d. 1152) of Germany joined the Crusade and led their respective armies toward Jerusalem in 1147 CE. However, they failed to win any major victories during this Crusade. During this Crusade they also laid a preemptive siege of Damascus, which failed. The city later fell into the hands of Nur ad-Din Zangi, who was a staunch enemy of the Crusaders. As a result of failure, the German and French kings returned to their homelands in 1150 CE.

d. Events Leading to the 3rd Crusade

After the failure of the 2nd crusade, Damascus and Syria came totally under the control of Nur ad-Din Zangi. Zangi also took control of Egypt by defeating the rulers, the Fatimid Dynasty. Zangi sent his most trusted General Shrikuh and his nephew Ṣalaḥ-ad-Din to conquer Egypt. Shirkuh died in 1169 CE and Nur ud-Din died five years later in 1174 CE, leaving the empire to his 11 year old son. It was then decided to hand over the ruling of the empire to Ṣalaḥ-ad-

Din who was considered more worthy of the position. Sultan Ṣalaḥ-ad-Din, as he was called later, had participated in many battles and was considered to be worthy enough to continue the war against the Crusaders. Sultan Ṣalaḥ-ad-Din also laid the foundations of the Ayyubid dynasty that ruled the Muslim areas for many years. The word **Ayyubid** is derived from the name "Ayyub", who was Ṣalaḥ-ad-Din's father and a soldier in the Zengid army.

Ṣalāḥ ad-Dīn Yūsuf ibn Ayyūbi (c. 1138 – March 4, 1193), has the distinction of being the first Ayyubid Sultan of Egypt and Syria. Sultan Ṣalaḥ-ad-Din was known to be a strict Sunni Muslim and many Muslims until today consider him to be the personification of the word 'chivalry'. His leadership qualities came to the forefront and he soon had his power all over Mesopotamia, Hejaz and Yemen along with Egypt and Syria. Ṣalaḥ-ad-Din was a Kurdish Muslim and after coming to power, he recaptured Palestine by leading his forces against the Crusaders. His victory in the **Battle of Hattin** was known to be a turning point in history and was marked by the removal of the Crusader Kingdom of Jerusalem from Palestine.

e. The Third Crusade (1187-1192)

When Ṣalaḥ-ad-Din conquered Jerusalem in 1187 CE, it created a shockwave all over Europe. A tax called "**The Saladin tithe**" was

43

levied in England and to some extent in France in 1188, in response to the capture of Jerusalem by Ṣalaḥ-ad-Din in 1187. **Pope Gregory VIII** (Alberto di Morra, b. 1100/1105 – d. 1187), therefore, called for yet another Crusade to recover Jerusalem from Ṣalaḥ-ad-Din.

The leaders of the Third Crusade were Europe's most important figures: **Philip II** of France (Philippe Auguste, b. 1165 – d. 1223), **Frederick I** of the Holy Roman Empire (Frederick I Barbarossa, b. 1122 – d. 1190) and **Henry II** of England. Later, after the death of Henry II, the English contingent came under the rule of **Richard I** of England (Coer de Lion/**Richard the Lionheart**, b. 1157 – d. 1199).

Like the previous Crusade, this attempt to recapture Jerusalem did not bear much fruit. However, other cities were captured by the Crusaders. The Roman Emperor Frederick I died by drowning in Cilicia in 1190. Richard, however, was able to capture the island of Cyprus and the City of Acre, but the Muslims eventually recaptured Acre in 1191. As a result, Philip decided to return to France in the same year Acre fell to the Muslims. Although the Crusaders were able to capture a lot of land, they were unable to take control of Jerusalem. Richard then entered into a treaty with Ṣalaḥ-ad-Din by which Jerusalem would remain under Muslim control and unarmed Christian pilgrims would be allowed to visit the city. Richard, therefore, returned to Europe without capturing Jerusalem.

One of Ṣalaḥ-ad-Din's distinctions is that despite his win over the Crusaders, the Crusaders held a high opinion of Ṣalaḥ-ad-Din and he gained the respect of many of his enemies like Richard the Lionheart. In fact when Richard had locked horns with Salah-ud-Din to regain control of Jerusalem, Richard and Salah-ud-Din, despite being military rivals, developed chivalrous mutual respect. In an offer to unite Christians and Muslims, Richard suggested to Salah-ud-Din to arrange the marriage of his brother (al-Adil) with Richard's daughter, Joan of England, Queen of Sicily, and recommended to make them both rulers of Jerusalem. Although that never materialized because both Joan and al-Adil refused to marry someone outside their faith,[29] it showed the respect that Richard had for his rival.

f. The Fourth Crusade (1202-1204)

Although the Crusaders were largely successful during the Third Crusade, their failure to recapture Jerusalem would lead to the call for a Fourth Crusade six years later. **Pope Innocent III** (Lotario dei Conti di Segni, b. 1160/1161 – d. 1216) initiated the Fourth Crusade with the primary intention of recapturing the Holy Land by passing through Egypt. This Crusade was one of the last of the major Crusades to be launched by the Papacy, though it quickly fell out of Papal control.

---

[29] Joan of England, Queen of Sicily -
http://en.wikipedia.org/wiki/Joan_of_England,_Queen_of_Sicily

During this Crusade, in April 1204, the Crusaders instead invaded the Christian Eastern Orthodox City of Constantinople, the capital of the Greek Byzantine Empire. The Crusaders established the so-called Latin Empire in Constantinople that resulted in minor crusades throughout the entire Greek empire. The Fourth Crusade is thus also known to have led to the **Great Schism**. Also referred to as the **East-West Schism**, this had resulted in the split of medieval Christianity into the **Eastern Orthodox Church** and **Western Roman Catholic Church** in 1054 CE. The reasons for the split were rooted both in political and theological disputes and are out of the scope of this e-book.

g. The Fifth Crusade (1217-1221)

In 1213 CE, **Pope Innocent III** issued the **papal bull**[30] calling all of Christendom to join a new Crusade to recapture Jerusalem and other parts of the Holy Land from the Muslims. The pope formulated a strategic plan that first aimed the conquering of the Ayyubid state in Egypt. In 1219 CE, the Crusader forces managed to capture the port of Damietta in Egypt. However, later as the Crusaders planned to attack Cairo in July 1221 CE, they decided to retreat as they were running low on supplies. The ruler of Egypt, **Ayyubid Sultan Al-Kamil** (b. 1180 – d. 1238), planned a night attack against the Crusaders that resulted in many Crusader losses and the eventual surrender by the Crusaders. The terms of the surrender called for

---

[30] "Papal bulls" used to be issued by the pope for communications of a public nature. However, after the fifteenth century, they were used only for the most formal or solemn occasions.

Al-Kamil to release the prisoners in return for the Crusaders relinquishing control of Damietta. After this Crusade, Al-Kamil also entered in a peace agreement with Europe for eight years.

h. The Sixth Crusade (1228-1229)

In 1228, **Pope Gregory IX** expelled **Emperor Fredrick II** (b. 1194 – d. 1250) from the Catholic Church for his repeated failures to live up to his promise to launch a Crusade to recover the Holy Land from the Muslim rulers. Despite being excommunicated, Frederick went to Jerusalem and was able to take control of Jerusalem, Nazareth and Bethlehem for about ten years. In 1229, Frederick II failed to conquer Egypt. As a result, he made peace with the Egypt ruler Sultan Al-Kamil. The treaty would give Christians power over Jerusalem, while the Muslims would have control over the Dome of the Rock and the Al-Aqsa Mosque. With this, Frederick had set a precedence by demonstrating to the Christians that a Crusade could be successful without military superiority or papal support. Further Crusades, therefore, would be launched by individual kings causing a further erosion of papal authority.

Later, after a lot of pressure from the Muslims, Al-Kamil repossessed Jerusalem in 1244 CE.

i. The Seventh Crusade (1248-1254)

This Crusade lasted from 1248 CE to 1254 CE and was a great failure for the Crusaders. The Seventh Crusade was led by *French King Louis IX* (b. 1214 – d. 1270) along with thousands of his troops. But through the combined efforts of the Sultan of Egypt, Ayyubid Sultan Turanshah, and his supporters, the Bahariyya Mamluks led by Emir Faris ad-Din Aktai of the Bahri Dynasty, Baibars al-Bunduqdari (who later became the Mamluk Sultan of Egypt, b. 1223 – d. 1277), Qutuz (the third of the Mamluk Sultan of Egypt, d. 1260), Aybak (who was the first Mamluk Sultan of Egypt, d. 1257) and Qalawun (the seventh Mamluk Sultan of Egypt, b. 1222 – d. 1290), King Louis IX was defeated and eventually captured. After paying a pricy ransom, he was finally released.

j. The Eight Crusade (1270)

Again in 1270, King Louis IX of France organized yet another crusade, the Eighth Crusade (though other scholars believe that this Crusade belongs to the Ninth). The original plan was to go to Syria, but the crusade was diverted to Tunis where Louis died. He was later canonized (made a saint) by the Catholic Church for his efforts. He was the only canonized king of France. Many places were named after him, most notably *São Luís do Maranhão, Brazil*, *St. Louis, Missouri*, in the United States and both the state and the city of *San Luis Potosí, in Mexico*.

k. The Ninth Crusade (1271-1272)

This crusade, like many others, also ended up in failure. It was the last major attempt of the Christian Latin Church to capture Jerusalem and the Holy Land from the Muslims rulers. The two previous attempts of King Louis IX of France to conquer Jerusalem from the Mamluks were enough for Prince Edward of England (who later became Edward I, b.1239 – d.1307) to launch yet another Crusade. The failure of this Crusade was a final blow to the crusading spirit of many and all support for launching more Crusades was lost. Furthermore, the Mamluk rulers in Egypt had also grown in power. Eventually, the remaining Crusader strongholds also fell to the Muslims: Antioch in 1268, Tripoli in 1289, and Acre in 1291.

6. World Zionist Organization (WZO) – From the "Holy Lands" to Israel

The World Zionist Organization (WZO) was founded in Basle, Switzerland, in 1897 by *Theodor Herzl* (b. 1860 – d. 1904), an Austro-Hungarian journalist. This was about twenty years before the end of the Ottoman Empire, which saw its decline in 1916 CE. The primary objective of WZO was the establishment of a Jewish homeland in Palestine. In 1896, Herzl published a paper entitled *Der Judenstaat* (The Jewish State) in which he elaborated that the only solution to the anti-Semitism that had increased in Europe was to establish the Jewish State in the areas of Palestine.

Herzl used to record his thoughts and ideas in a diary that became public later. Some of what he wrote in his diaries shows the progression of his thoughts and ideas about making a separate homeland for the Jewish people. The following are some excerpts from his diaries and his book "The Jewish State".

After the first Basle Congress held in 1897 (more than 50 years before the founding of the state of Israel), Theodor Herzl wrote in his diary:[31]

> *"Were I to sum up the Basle Congress in a word – which I shall guard against pronouncing publicly – it would be this: 'At Basle, I founded the Jewish State. If I said this out loud today, I would be answered by*

---

[31] Jewish Virtual Library -
http://www.jewishvirtuallibrary.org/jsource/Zionism/firstcong.html

50

universal laughter. If not in 5 years, certainly in 50, everyone will know it.'"

In the paper **Der Judenstaat** (The Jewish State), Herzl wrote:

"And what glory awaits those who fight unselfishly for the cause! Therefore I believe that a wondrous generation of Jews will spring into existence. The Maccabeans will rise again. Let me repeat once more my opening words: The Jews who wish for a State will have it. We shall live at last as free men on our own soil, and die peacefully in our own homes. The world will be freed by our liberty, enriched by our wealth, magnified by our greatness. And whatever we attempt there to accomplish for our own welfare, will react powerfully and beneficially for the good of humanity."

Herzl also wrote in his diary the following:

"One day, when the Jewish state will be in existence, everything will appear petty and self-evident. Perhaps a fair-minded historian will find that it was something, after all, that an impecunious Jewish journalist, in the midst of the deepest degradation of the Jewish people and at a time of the most disgusting anti-Semitism, made a flag out of a rag and a people out of a decadent rabble, and was able to rally this people around such a flag (June 1, 1901, Diaries, 3: 1151)."[32]

---

[32] The Jewish State - 1896, Theodor Herzl's Program for Zionism - http://www.zionism-israel.com/js/Jewish_State.html

It is clear from the above how Herzl established himself as the father of the Zionist movement that later was instrumental in issuing the Balfour Declaration (covered later in this book) and then eventually the creation of the state of Israel with Jerusalem as its official capital.

Originally named *"Zionist Organization"* since its foundation in 1897, the group was later renamed as **World Zionist Organization** (WZO) in 1960 to give it worldwide visibility. The WZO is governed by the supreme institution called the **Zionist Congress**. The Zionist constitution was passed by the third congress in 1899 and remains in effect until today, despite many amendments. The entire WZO is managed by elected officials, the Zionist General Council and the Zionist Executive. The Zionist Organization has an independent law court, an attorney and a comptroller. The head of the Zionist Executive also functions as the chairman and the president of the World Zionist Organization.

The World Zionist Organization (WZO) was very instrumental in the declaration of the statement issued by British Foreign Secretary *Sir Arthur James Balfour*, known today as the *Balfour Declaration*. The objective of the Balfour Declaration was a reiteration of the very objective of the WZO, which was **"to establish a home for the Jewish people in Palestine, secured under public law."**[33] The declaration was in the form of a letter issued by the British Foreign Secretary to **Baron Rothschild** (Walter Rothschild, 2nd Baron Rothschild), a leader of the British Jewish community, for

---

[33] "World Zionist Organization (WZO)." Jewish Virtual Library, n.d. Web, retrieved on 19 June 2010.

transmission to the Zionist Federation of Great Britain and Ireland. The letter reflected the position of the British Cabinet regarding Jews wishing to form their own homeland in Palestine, as agreed upon in a meeting on 31 October 1917. It further stated that the declaration is a sign of **"sympathy with Jewish Zionist aspirations."**

The following is the complete text of the Balfour Declaration issued by British Foreign Secretary Sir James Arthur Balfour in November 2, 1917:

Foreign Office,

2 November 1917

Dear Lord Rothschild,

I have much pleasure in conveying to you, on behalf of His Majesty's Government, the following declaration of sympathy with the Jewish Zionist aspirations which has been submitted to, and approved by, the Cabinet.

His Majesty's Government view with favour the establishment in Palestine of a national home for the Jewish people, and will use their best endeavours to facilitate the achievement of this project, it being clearly understood that nothing shall be done which may prejudice the civil and religious rights of the existing non-Jewish communities in Palestine, or the rights and political status enjoyed by Jews in any other country.

I should be grateful if you would bring this declaration to the knowledge of the Zionist Federation.

Yours sincerely,

Arthur James Balfour

The influence that the WZO enjoyed at the time is quite clear in the declaration. However, the Balfour Declaration created a certain amount of controversy and not all Jews took this declaration positively, especially those Jewish individuals who were against the objectives of the WZO to establish an exclusive Jewish homeland in Palestine. To understand the ideology about Jews who don't support Zionism, the organization called *"True Torah Jews against Zionism"* provides the following description about themselves on their website:[34]

> *"The relatively new concept of Zionism began only about one hundred years ago and since that time Torah-true Jewry has steadfastly opposed the Zionist ideology. This struggle is rooted in two convictions:*
>
> - *Zionism, by advocating a political and military end to the Jewish exile, denies the very essence of our Diaspora existence. We are in exile by Divine Decree and may emerge from exile solely via Divine Redemption. All human efforts to alter a metaphysical reality are doomed to end in failure and bloodshed. History has clearly borne out this teaching.*
>
> - *Zionism has not only denied our fundamental belief in Heavenly Redemption it has also created*

---

[34] http://jewsagainstzionism.com/

a pseudo-Judaism which views the essence of our identity to be a secular nationalism. Accordingly, Zionism and the Israeli state have consistently endeavored, via persuasion and coercion, to replace a Divine and Torah centered understanding of our people hood with an armed materialism.

True Torah Jews are dedicated to informing the world and in particular the American public and politicians that all Jews do not support the ideology of the Zionist state called "Israel" which is diametrically opposite to the teachings of traditional Judaism."

After the issuance of the Balfour Declaration, the Palestinians clearly felt that their rights had been violated by the declaration of the creation of a Jewish state in Palestine. In the end, the Balfour Declaration greatly favored the Jews in general as in the years following the issue of the Balfour Declaration, a great number of Jews returned to the land of Palestine to fulfill the **Aliyah** or the **Law of Return**. With the migration of thousands of Jews to Palestine, this precipitated the declaring of the state of Israel as an independent nation.

7. The British Mandate for Palestine and the Creation of Israel

"Palestine" started to slip away from the hands of Muslim Ottoman rule after their defeat at the hands of the British in 1917 during World War I. When the British emerged victorious over the Ottoman Turks in World War I, the British soldiers had also taken control of Jerusalem. This British occupation in Palestine lasted for approximately thirty-one years – from December 1917 to May 1948 when Jerusalem was divided into two. The British soldiers who had captured Jerusalem from the Turks were led by **General Sir Edmund Allenby** (b. 1861 – d. 1936). Edmund Allenby was the British Commander who led the Egyptian Expeditionary Force to capture Jerusalem on 9th December 1917.

After the takeover, the city was very impoverished and inhabited by various ethnic groups. As Great Britain started to govern the Palestinian lands, they made certain improvements to the infrastructure in Jerusalem. The British rulers implemented an overhaul of the city by requiring new buildings through strategic town planning. The aim was to preserve the overall look of the city and its rich historical past.

With the start of the British rule, however, the political situation involving Arabs and the Jews started to deteriorate. One of the reasons was the dual but conflicting support that British had provided to the Zionist organization as well as to **Emir Faisal I** (Faisal bin al-Hussein bin Ali al-Hashemi and not to be confused with King Faisal of Saudi-Arabia who came much later). Emir Faisal was the king of the Arab Kingdom of Syria or Greater Syria and later became the king of the Kingdom of Iraq. Emir Faisal had earlier joined hands with the British Army to fight the Ottoman Empire in an effort to get Arabs gain control of the Arab regions that were under the Ottoman rule. He was given a pledge by the British that the Arab areas (including Jerusalem and other Palestinian areas) will be returned to Arab control. However, this conflicted with the Balfour Declaration, which showed British support to the Zionists and thus sent a conflicting message that in turn made matters quite complex. This is because the Balfour declaration triggered an en masse migration of Jews back to the Palestinian lands. This complicated situation is reflected in the statement that **Lord Curzon**[35] made in the meeting of the British Cabinet on December 5, 1918. Lord Curzon stated the following:

> *'The Palestine position is this. If we deal with our commitments, there is first the general pledge to Hussein in October 1915, under which Palestine was included in the areas as to which Great Britain pledged itself that they should be Arab and independent in the future . . . Great Britain and France - Italy subsequently agreeing - committed themselves to an international administration of Palestine in consultation with Russia, who was an ally at that time . . . A new feature was brought into the case in November 1917, when Mr Balfour, with the authority of the War Cabinet, issued his famous declaration to the Zionists that Palestine 'should be the national home of the Jewish people, but that nothing should be done - and this, of course, was*

---

[35] Lord Curzon was a British Conservative statesman who was Viceroy of India and Foreign Secretary.

a most important proviso - to prejudice the civil and religious rights of the existing non-Jewish communities in Palestine. Those, as far as I know, are the only actual engagements into which we entered with regard to Palestine.

Now, as regards the facts, they are these. First, Palestine has been conquered by the British, with only very insignificant aid from small French and Italian contingents, and it is now being administered by the British. The Zionist declaration of our Government has been followed by a very considerable immigration of Jews. One of the difficulties of the situation arises from the fact that the Zionists have taken full advantage - and are disposed to take even fuller advantage - of the opportunity which was then offered to them. You have only to read, as probably most of us do, their periodical 'Palestine', and, indeed, their pronouncements in the papers, to see that their programme is expanding from day to day. They now talk about a Jewish State. The Arab portion of the population is well-nigh forgotten and is to be ignored. They not only claim the boundaries of the old Palestine, but they claim to spread across the Jordan into the rich countries lying to the east, and, indeed, there seems to be very small limit to the aspirations which they now form. The Zionist programme, and the energy with which it is being carried out, have not unnaturally had the consequence of arousing the keen suspicions of the Arabs. By 'the Arabs' I do not merely mean Feisal and his followers at Damascus, but the so-called Arabs who inhabit the country. There seems, from the telegrams we receive, to be growing up an increasing friction between the two communities, a feeling by the Arabs that we are really behind the Zionists and not behind the Arabs, and altogether a situation which is becoming rather critical . . .

Later, it became clear that Lord Curzon had laid out the British government's position and explained that:

> *Palestine was included in the areas as to which Great Britain pledged itself that they should be Arab and independent in the future.*[36]

In 1919, Faisal attended the **Paris Peace Conference** in an effort to get Arabs control the Arab areas that were previously under the Ottoman Empire. The conference was held by the Allied victors following the end of World War I to set the peace terms for Germany and other defeated nations (including the Ottoman Empire). During the conference, the Zionist Organization had submitted their draft plan, which was followed by the Conference's decision that the former Arab provinces of the Ottoman Empire would be separated from it and the newly conceived mandate-system applied to them. During the conference, Emir Faisal and **Dr. Chaim Weizmann** (President of the World Zionist Organization) signed what came to be known as the Faisal–Weizmann Agreement for Arab-Jewish cooperation. In this agreement, Faisal conditionally accepted the Balfour Declaration based on the fulfillment of British wartime promises and he made the following statement:

> *We Arabs... look with the deepest sympathy on the Zionist movement. Our deputation here in Paris is fully acquainted with the proposals submitted yesterday by the Zionist Organization to the Peace Conference, and*

---

[36] http://en.wikipedia.org/wiki/Faisal-Weizmann_Agreement

we regard them as moderate and proper. We will do our best, in so far as we are concerned, to help them through; we will wish the Jews a most hearty welcome home... I look forward, and my people with me look forward, to a future in which we will help you and you will help us, so that the countries in which we are mutually interested may once again take their places in the community of the civilized peoples of the world.[37]

There were, however, numerous disagreements and misinterpretations to the various agreements that were in motion during that time. For example, Dr. Chaim Weizmann wrote in his autobiography *Trial and Error* that Palestine had been excluded from the areas that should have been Arab and independent.[38]

During the conference, Chaim Weizmann presented its case together with a map of the proposed country. The statement supported the creation of a mandate entrusted to Britain and stated the Jewish historical connection with the area. This therefore resulted in the issuance of the *British Mandate for Palestine*. It was also at the Paris Peace Conference that the name "Palestine" was applied to refer to the territories entrusted to Great Britain. The British Mandate for Palestine comprised of the territories of what is modern-day Israel and Jordan.[39]

---

[37] http://en.wikipedia.org/wiki/Faisal-Weizmann_Agreement

[38] *Trial and Error: The Autobiography of Chaim Weizmann*. Chaim Weizmann. Greenwood Pub Group (June 1972).

[39] The term "Palestinian" was used when the Palestinian National Authority was established to refer to its citizens. During this time Palestine was used to refer to the entire "Holy Land."

The primary objective of the creation of the British Mandate for Palestine was to fulfill the dream of the World Zionist Organization in helping to establish a Jewish homeland in the land of Palestine as engraved in the Balfour Declaration of 1917. The mandate was later ratified by Article 22 of the Covenant of the League of Nations.[40] Under Article 22, it was specified *"that the territories inhabited by peoples unable to stand by themselves would be entrusted to advanced nations until such time as the local population could handle their own affairs."[41]*

During the British rule, there was increasing unrest from the Arab population who clearly opposed the high number of Jewish immigrants flooding to Jerusalem to fulfill the Aliyah (the return of Jews to the Jewish lands). The unrest, characterized by riots, continued from the 1920s until the 1930s. The growing unrest was also characterized by killings on all sides and destructions all over Jerusalem. The level of violence continued to escalate throughout the 1940s and a vast number of civilians were affected. The authority that Britain had on Palestine, therefore, was increasingly getting weaker. The British government was also experiencing public relation issues because Britain was stopping Jews who had survived the holocaust from entering Palestine. The reason for limiting Jewish migration to Palestine was obviously the increasing stiff Arab resistance. Additionally, Britain's sinking economy from the

[40] The League of Nations (LON) was an intergovernmental organization whose primary goals included preventing war through collective security, disarmament, and settling international disputes through negotiation and arbitration. However, during the onset of the Second World War, Germany withdrew from the League, soon to be followed by many other aggressive powers. The war showed that the League had failed its primary purpose, which was to avoid

[41] See "The Balfour Declaration of 1917." Wikipedia, n.d. Web, retrieved on 19 June 2010.

effects of World War II and the economic and political pressure in maintaining approximately 100,000 men in Palestine eventually pushed the British government to end their rule in Palestine.

These events then led to the United Nations (UN) General Assembly to certify a plan on November 29, 1947 (Resolution 181), dividing the British Mandate for Palestine into two states: one Jewish and one Arab. Jerusalem, however, was to be designated as an international city to be administered by the UN. This plan was accepted by the entire Jewish community. The Arabs, however, clearly feeling that their lands were taken away from them, rejected it and continued their resistance. On May 14, 1948, the day before the British rule would officially end, Israel declared independence and elected **David Ben-Gurion** (b. 1886 – d. 1973) as the first Israeli Prime Minister. He was the Prime Minister from May 14, 1948 until January 24, 1954 (Later, Ben-Gurion would again serve as Prime Minister from November 3, 1955 to June 26, 1963).

The day after Israel declared its independence, four of Israel's Arab neighbors (Egypt, Syria, Lebanon and Iraq) declared war against the new state. The war would later be known as the *War of Independence in Israel.*

8. The "Aliyah" (Jewish Immigration to Israel)

The fulfillment of Aliyah was one of the major objectives of Zionism and is deeply anchored in Judaism. The concept of Aliyah was derived from the Biblical image of the Jews in the Diaspora (exiled) who, as individuals or groups, were arriving and returning to live in *Eretz Yisrael* (Land of Israel). The modern usage of Aliyah refers to the absorption of Jews from other parts of the world into the mainstream Jewish society in Israel. Aliyah originally signified the "ascension" or "going up" of the children of Israel to Egypt as mentioned in the Jewish text Genesis 50:14 and Numbers 32:11. Later in history, Aliyah came to signify the return of the children of Israel to their homeland from captivity in Babylon as mentioned in the Jewish text Ezra 2:1 and 59. Today, the term "Aliyah" simply means the migration of Jews to Eretz Yisrael (Land of Israel).

The following are the Jewish texts referring to Aliyah:

"After Joseph had buried his father he returned to Egypt, together with his brothers and all who had gone up with him for the burial of his father." (Genesis 50:14)

"Because they have not followed me unreservedly, none of these men of twenty years or more who have come up from Egypt shall ever see this country I promised under oath to Abraham and Isaac and Jacob..." (Numbers 32:11)

"These are the inhabitants of the province who returned from the captivity of the exiles, whom Nebuchadnezzar, king of Babylon, had carried away to Babylon, and who came back to Jerusalem and Judah, each man in his own city...(Ezra 2:1)

"The following who returned from Tel-melah, Tel-harsha, Cherub, Addan, and Immer were unable to prove that their ancestral houses and their descent were Israelite...(Ezra 2:59)

The earliest wave of Jews who returned to Eretz Yisrael happened in the Biblical times when the Kingdom of Judah fell apart and approximately 50,000 Jews returned to their homeland from the Babylonian exile. Afterwards, history witnessed a number of occasions when Jews returned to the Land of Israel after being expelled from it. The following summarizes some of those periods of Aliyah when Jews returned to the lands of Palestine / Israel.

a. The First Aliyah (1882-1903)

The first known Aliyah of recent times took place in the period from 1882 until 1903 when the Jews from the Russian Empire started immigrating to Palestine, then a province of the Ottoman Empire. The majority of those Jews belonged to the *Hovevei Zion and Bilu movements.*[42] A small number of Jews also came from Yemen. When they arrived in Palestine, many of them started working in

---

[42] These movements' aim was to promote Jewish immigration to the Land of Israel.

agricultural fields, and as a result of their increasing numbers, new towns sprung up. The Russian Jews established themselves in towns that included Petah Tikva, Rishon LeZion, Rosh Pina and Zikhron Ya'aqov. The Yemenite Jews, on the other hand, settled in the Arab suburb of Jerusalem known as Silwan.

b. The Second Aliyah (1904-1914)

The period of the second Aliyah of recent times was from 1904 to 1914, when about 40,000 Jews immigrated to Palestine, again from Russia. However, the major factor driving Aliyah during these years was the outbreak of pogroms (riots) due to the rise of anti-Semitism feelings in Russia. It was during this period that the suburb of Jaffa, Ahuzat Bayit, was established, and later on grew into what is Tel Aviv City today. It was also during this time that Hebrew was revived as the national language in Israel.

c. The Third Aliyah (1919-1923)

When the First World War ended, a group of 40,000 Jews from the Russian Empire arrived in Palestine from 1919 to 1923. This Aliyah was different from the earlier ones as this migration was influenced by the Zionist motivations of setting up a Jewish homeland in the lands of Palestine. As mentioned earlier, it was during this time that Great Britain conquered Palestine from the Ottoman Empire and Sir

Arthur James Balfour issued the Balfour declaration showing British support for the creation of the Jewish homeland in Palestine.

d. The Fourth Aliyah (1924-1929)

During the period from 1924 to 1929, anti-Semitism feelings were rising to alarming levels in certain European countries such as Poland and Hungary. This resulted in a fourth wave of Aliyah. Majority of the Jews who arrived in Palestine during this Aliyah were thus from Europe. It was during this time that the United States had implemented immigration quotas, which also kept European Jews from immigrating to the US.

e. The Fifth Aliyah (1929-1939)

As the wave of Nazism rose in Germany in the 1920s, around 250,000 German Jews fled the country and immigrated to Palestine in the period from 1929 to 1939. Due to the large number of Jews coming to Palestine, the British implemented a stringent measure against the increasing number of Jews from Eastern Europe. The immigration beyond approved quotas was referred to as the **Aliyah Bet**. In this wave of Aliyah, majority of the Jews were professionals from Germany such as doctors, lawyers, and professors. In 1940, the Jewish population in Palestine reached 450,000. It was also during this period that Arabs started reacting against the large number of Jews and the land of Palestine saw an increase in the number of Jewish / Arab riots.

Although the above are known as the five specific periods of Aliyah, the continued migration of Jews from other parts of the world continued to add to the Jewish population in Palestine. Jews immigrated in large numbers from Iran, Yemen, Ethiopia, Argentina, France, as well as North America. Although the fifth Aliyah marked the end of the large wave of Jewish immigration to the lands of Palestine, Jews continued to return to Israel until the 1990s and many are even immigrating back to Israel today.

Today, Aliyah continues as Jews from all over the world return and / or visit Israel. In fact, the Israeli government recommends that the best age for Aliyah is when a Jew is younger, at least 22 years old, since it is easier for the person to learn Hebrew. Finally, in order to accommodate the growing number of Jews who are returning or visiting Israel, the *Jewish Agency for Israel* (JAFI) has established the *Israel Aliyah Center*. JAFI lists the following introduction about itself on its website:

> *"As the authentic global Jewish partnership, the Jewish Agency has brought the Jewish world together since 1929 to do the impossible: Building the State of Israel; bringing 3 million Jews home."*

9. Major Israeli Conflicts

After the end of the Crusades, the Holy Land enjoyed peace for many centuries (starting from the 13th century) until World War I, when the British conquered Jerusalem. It was at this time that Jewish immigration hit its peak. This started many Arab and Israeli conflicts that continued until after the founding of Israel. The following lists some of the major conflicts.

a. The "Great Arab Revolt" in Palestine (1936 – 1939)

Between 1936 and 1939, after the British police killed **Shaykh Izz ad-Din al-Qassam** near Jenin in November 1935, the Arabs sparked off a rebellion for their expression of strong disagreement with the British government and the majority of Jewish immigrants.

The British reacted to the war by increasing their military forces and by taking a strict action against the Arabs that included curfews, house demolitions, imprisonment without charges or trial and more. However, the primary form of punishment employed by the British was demolition of houses that in some cases included complete decimation of Arab communities. In many instances, this method was criticized even by the senior British leaders themselves. One example is that of **Palestine Chief Justice Sir Michael McDonnell** who criticized such British tactics. This resulted in his removal from his position and the area. During this revolt, according to official

British figures covering the whole revolt, the British army and police killed more than 2,000 Arabs in combat, and 108 were hanged after trials. Other statistics put the Arab death at more than 5000 with scores of casualties.[43] During this period, the British also unofficially sided with *"The Haganah"*, which was an unofficial Jewish paramilitary organization. The Haganah, along with two other paramilitary groups called *Lehi* and *Irgun* operating in the British Mandate of Palestine, later merged to become the *Israel Defense Forces (IDF)*, which today is the military force of the state of Israel.

Although the rebel's direct aims and objectives in this conflict were not met, this highlighted the face of the Arab Palestinian conflict.

b. 1948 Arab-Israeli War

This war is also referred to as *The War of Independence* or *War of Liberation* by the Israelis. This war had actually commenced toward the end of the British Mandate of Palestine in 1947 after the UN General Assembly's Resolution 181 that would have created two states — Arab and Jewish — side by side. The declaration of independence by the Jews essentially pushed the surrounding five Arab countries of Egypt, Syria, Transjordan (later Jordan), Iraq and Lebanon to wage war against Israel. The acceptance of the notion of the creation of a Jewish homeland in Palestine was simply unacceptable to the Arab powers simply because the territory declared as Israel was considered to be an Arab territory.

---

[43] http://en.wikipedia.org/wiki/1936%E2%80%931939_Arab_revolt_in_Palestine

As the war progressed,[44] Egyptians were able to acquire some portions of Israeli territory in the south while the Jordanians captured the old city of Jerusalem. However, these advances were short-lived. In June 1948, the United Nations issued a four-week truce. In the following month, the Israeli forces made successful advances, resulting in the eruption of another war in August that lasted until the end of 1948. On January 7, 1949, isolated Egyptian forces were forced to declare a ceasefire. The armistice agreement between Israel and Egypt, Syria, and Jordan resulted in the declaration of a ceasefire, but not a formal peace agreement. As the war ended, a little more than 700,000 Palestinian Arabs were displaced and more than 400 Arab villages were depopulated. This also included about ten Jewish villages and neighborhoods. Most Arabs escaped Israel and settled in refugee camps near the border. The status became a volatile factor in Arab-Israeli relations.

As this war was a flash point between the relationship of Jews and Arabs, the events of this war are contested to this date by historians on both sides.

c. The Sinai Campaign of 1956 (Operation Kadesh)

---

[44] The militarization of the Israeli armed forces started as early as 1936 when the British government facilitated the recruitment, training, arming and funding of security and intelligence forces for the Jewish Agency, the pre-state government before the independence of Israel. The British military's facilitation on Jewish recruits continued until the end of the British rule in Palestine in 1948. By the time the British rule slowly declined, the Jewish forces were already established and trained by the British armed forces.

Conditions became relatively peaceful when the United Nations enforced a truce between Israel and the Arabs. This, however, lasted only until 1956 when tensions grew again between the Arab states and Israel. The world superpowers became involved when the United States, Great Britain and France sided with Israel, while the Soviet Union backed the Arabs. The involvement of the world's greatest powers was due to the fact that Egypt's Gamal Abdal Nasser nationalized the Suez Canal in July 1956. Four months later, on October 29, 1956, the Israeli forces along with Great Britain and France began a combined air and ground assault against Egypt's Sinai Peninsula. The Israeli assault was later backed up and reinforced by British and French forces, resulting in the Israeli invasion of the canal. The Israeli invasion along the canal also resulted in the capture of Gaza Strip and Sharm el Sheikh.

d. The Six-Day War (June 1967)

The issue related to occupied Arab territories in the land of Palestine continued the resentment between Israel and its neighbors. This escalated into a war that started on June 5, 1967 when Israel attacked Egypt, Jordan, and Syria. By the end of the war, Israel had managed to capture the Gaza Strip and the Sinai Peninsula from Egypt, the West Bank and East Jerusalem from Jordan, and the Golan Heights from Syria.

The superior air capability that Israel had managed to gather since its declaration of independence resulted in crippling the air defenses of Egypt, Syria, and Jordan. This war, therefore, established Israel's military supremacy in the region. Israel managed to seize East Jerusalem, Hebron, and the entire West Bank from Jordan for three days. The battle for Golan Heights with Syria lasted only two days, from June 9 to June 10.

This war was significant for Jews because for the first time in more than 2000 years, they had control over Jerusalem.

After this war, both sides assessed their strengths and weaknesses. Egypt attributed its loss to "the individualistic bureaucratic leadership;" "promotions on the basis of loyalty, not expertise, and the army's fear of telling Nasser the truth;" lack of intelligence; and better Israeli weapons, command, organization, and will to fight.[45] On the other hand, the then-Israeli Defense Minister Moshe Dayan listed several shortcomings in Israel's actions in his report to the Israeli general staff. Among others, he mentioned misinterpretation of Nasser's intentions, overdependence on the United States, and reluctance to act when Egypt earlier had closed the Straits.

e. The War of Attrition (1968-70)

The ongoing rift between Israel and Arabs pushed the Arab states to come up with a "Three NO's" policy in September 1967. The policy meant that there could be NO peace with Israel, NO Arab state will negotiate with Israel and Israel will NOT be recognized by the Arab states: thus, no peace, no recognition and no negotiation. Believing that only military action could compel Israel and the

---

[45] The Six Day War - http://en.wikipedia.org/wiki/Six-Day_War

international community to withdraw its forces from the Sinai, Egyptian President Gamel Abdel Nasser formally declared war against Israel on March 8, 1969. The war ended without Nasser achieving any of his objectives. The frontiers remained the same as they were before the war, and no peace agreements were negotiated.

f. The Yom Kippur War (October 1973)

The Yom Kippur War took place from 1973 to 1974 as a result of a carefully planned attack by the Arabs against Israel. This war is also called the Yom Kippur War because it was launched on the Jewish holiday of Yom Kippur. On the day of Yom Kippur, October 6, 1973, the Arab states led by Egyptian President Anwar Sadat launched an attack on Israel. Since the country was celebrating an important Jewish holiday, Israeli forces were caught off-guard. As a result, it took Israel many days to fully mobilize its armed forces.

Although the Arab states made a lot of headway in the early days of the war, most of their advances were reversed later. As before, the United States supported Israel and the Soviet Union supported the Arab states. This increased the tension between the two nuclear super powers.

As the war progressed, the United Nations along with the United States and the Soviet Union used diplomatic pressures for a ceasefire. Consequently, Israel and Egypt signed a ceasefire agreement in the following month of November 1973, but the

Syrians continued to fight with Israel until they negotiated a peace agreement in 1974.

g. The 1982 Lebanon War

The 1982 Lebanon war was also called **"Operation Peace for Galilee"**. As there were numerous Palestinian refugees living in southern Lebanon, there were continual border skirmishes between Israel and Lebanon. In 1982, therefore, Israel started launching air raids and then ultimately invaded southern Lebanon. The main objective was to push the Palestinian fighters further north in Lebanese territory. Israel attacked various military bases belonging to the Palestinian Liberation Organization (PLO) in Lebanon, resulting in the evacuation of Palestinians to various Arab countries.

h. The Sabra and Shatila Massacre (16 September 1982)

The Sabra and Shatila were former refugee camps used to shelter displaced Palestinians in West Beirut, Lebanon. On September 16, 1982, a massacre took place in Sabra and Shatilla that forever changed the image of the place which was primarily created to house, shelter and accommodate homeless Palestinians as well as Lebanese Muslim civilians. Later, this came to be known as the Sabra and Shatila massacre of 1982.

The root of the massacre can be traced to the death of Lebanese President Bachir Gemayel (b. 1947 – d. 1982), who was assassinated through an explosive device at the **Phalangist** headquarters in Beirut on September 14, 1982. The death of Gemayel, himself a commander of the Christian forces and leader of the Lebanese Social Democratic Party or Phalangist (**Phalanges** in French; **Kataeb** in Arabic), was later attributed to **Habib Shartouni**, who was a member of the Syrian Social Nationalist Party. The Phalanges was a Lebanese Christian militia group.

As a lot of hate simmered between the Lebanese Christian and Muslim groups, the Phalanges (the Lebanese Christian Groups) attacked the Muslim refugee camps assuming that the killers were hiding in those camps. At that time, the Israeli Defense Forces (IDF)—under the command of Israeli Defense minister **Ariel Sharon** and Chief of Staff Lieutenant **General Rafael Eitan** — had taken control of the refugee camps and allowed the Phalangists to enter two of the refugee camps, the Sabra and Shatila.[46] While inside the camps, the Phalangists started indiscriminately killing camp residents, in retaliation for their leader's assassination. The exact number of victims, which included women, children and babies, remained unknown and disputed. The Israeli intelligence sources reported that there were approximately 700 to 800 deaths; while international sources reported that there were about 3,500 victims. On September 18, 1982, the Lebanese Health Ministry along with the Lebanese soldiers uncovered the atrocities committed against

---

[46] Israel had openly supported the Lebanese Christian groups, which were also trained in Israel.

the civilians, including desecration of corpses, rapes and the destruction of houses.

The massacre in Sabra and Shatila immediately created a huge impact against the Israeli government. Massive rallies in Tel Aviv were organized to pressure Prime Minister Menachem Begin to conduct a thorough investigation against the Israeli forces failing to stop the killings in Lebanon's two refugee camps. Begin launched an investigative committee led by Supreme Court Chief Justice Yitzchak Kahan along with Supreme Court Justice Aharon Barak and Major General Yona Efrat as committee members.

The Israeli Kahan Commission released its findings of the massacre and attributed full responsibility of the massacre to the Phalangists (under the command of Elie Hobeika). On the other hand, the commission noted that the Israeli political and military leaders had a share of responsibility with respect to the deaths of the victims. The commission made no mention of the direct participation of Prime Minister Begin in the massacre, but stated that his *"non-involvement in the entire issue charges him with a certain amount of responsibility."* On the part of Defense Minister Ariel Sharon, the committee determined that his blame in the massacre was his failure to ignore the possibility of a massacre and by approving the Phalangists' entry into the Sabra and Shatila camps. The commission thus recommended the removal of Sharon from his position. Begin, later dismissed Sharon as the Minister of Defense. Like Sharon, Chief of Staff Lieutenant General Rafael Eitan was also found to have failed to prevent the massacre from occurring, but unlike Sharon, Eitan was allowed to finish his term as chief of staff.

In the same year (1982 CE), an independent international commission headed by Sean MacBride (b. 1904 – d. 1988), the former Irish Minister of Foreign Affairs, investigated the Sabra and Shatila massacre to determine the violations of Israel with respect to international law during its invasion of Lebanon. The MacBride commission released its report, entitled "Israel in Lebanon", finding Israel guilty of committing an aggression on Lebanon that was contrary to international law.

In 1983, an Israeli inquiry named **Hobeika** to have personally directed the Sabra and Shatila massacre. A few years later in June 2001, **Chibli Mallat**, a left-wing Maronite lawyer, filed a case against Ariel Sharon in Belgium under a law that allowed foreigners to be sued for crimes against humanity. Just before his death (assassinated in a car explosion), Hobeika had publicly declared his intention to testify against Sharon about Sharon's involvement in the Sabra and Shatila massacre in the Belgian court. A Belgian senator named Josy Dubié was quoted as saying that Hobeika had told him several days before his death that he had "revelations" to disclose about the massacres and felt "threatened". When Dubié had asked Hobeika about the reasons for not revealing all the facts immediately, Hobeika is reported to have said: "I am saving them for the trial." Subsequently, both Israelis and Arabs blamed each other for Hobeika's assassination claiming that the other party would have proven guilty during the trial for the massacre.[47]

---

[47] Sabra and Shatila Massacare -

i. The Gulf War (1991)

Though Israel did not directly participate in the Gulf War, the country did prepare for a possible confrontation with Iraq as Saddam Hussein issued threats "to burn half of Israel." As a result of the United State's pressure on Israel, the Israeli government tried to stay out of the conflict fearing that their involvement could change the dynamics of Arabs' stance on the war.

10. The Concept of 'Greater Israel'

The "Greater Israel" is a modern and ambitious political concept that aims to reestablish and recapture the original Biblical land mass of ancient Israel. The concept of Greater Israel is primarily based on religious writings found in the Jewish texts. The basis of Greater Israel is found in Genesis 15:18-21, Number 34:1-15 and Ezekiel 47:13-20.

> ### Genesis 15:18-20
>
> *It was on that occasion that the LORD made a covenant with Abram, saying: "To your descendants I give this land, from the Wadi of Egypt to the Great River (the Euphrates), the land of the Kenites, the Kenizzites, the Kadmonites, the Hittites, the Perizzites, the Rephaim, the Amorites, the Canaanites, the Girgashites, and the Jebusites."*
>
> ### Number 34:1-15
>
> *The LORD said to Moses, "Give the Israelites this order: When you enter the land of Canaan, this is the territory that shall fall to you as your heritage--the land of Canaan with its boundaries:*
>
> *"Your southern boundary shall be at the desert of Zin along the border of Edom; on the east it shall begin at the end of the Salt Sea, and turning south of the Akrabbim Pass, it shall cross Zin, and extend south of Kadesh-barnea to Hazar-addar; thence it shall cross to Azmon, and turning from Azmon to the Wadi of Egypt, shall terminate at the Sea.*

"For your western boundary you shall have the Great Sea with its coast; this shall be your western boundary.

"The following shall be your boundary on the north: from the Great Sea you shall draw a line to Mount Hor, and shall continue it from Mount Hor to Labo in the land of Hamath, with the boundary extending through Zedad. Thence the boundary shall reach to Ziphron and terminate at Hazar-enan. This shall be your northern boundary.

"For your eastern boundary you shall draw a line from Hazar-enan to Shepham. From Shepham the boundary shall go down to Ar-Baal, east of Ain, and descending further, shall strike the ridge on the east side of the Sea of Chinnereth; thence the boundary shall continue along the Jordan and terminate with the Salt Sea.

"This is the land that shall be yours, with the boundaries that surround it."

Moses also gave this order to the Israelites: "This is the land, to be apportioned among you by lot, which the LORD has commanded to be given to the nine and one half tribes. For all the ancestral houses of the tribe of Reuben, and the ancestral houses of the tribe of Gad, as well as half of the tribe of Manasseh, have already received their heritage; these two and one half tribes have received their heritage on the eastern side of the Jericho stretch of the Jordan, toward the sunrise."

Ezekiel 47:13-20

> *Thus says the Lord GOD: These are the boundaries*
> *within which you shall apportion the land among the*
> *twelve tribes of Israel (Joseph having two portions). All*
> *of you shall have a like portion in this land which I*
> *swore to give to your fathers, that it might fall to you*
> *as your inheritance. This is the boundary of the land*
> *on the north side: from the Great Sea in the direction*
> *of Hethlon, past Labo of Hamath, to Zedad, Berothah,*
> *and Sibraim, along the frontiers of Hamath and*
> *Damascus, to Hazar-enon which is on the border of the*
> *Hauran. Thus the border shall extend from the sea to*
> *Hazar-enon, with the frontier of Hamath and Damascus*
> *to the north. This is the northern boundary. The*
> *eastern boundary: between the Hauran--toward*
> *Damascus--and Gilead on the one side, and the land of*
> *Israel on the other side, the Jordan shall form the*
> *boundary down to the eastern sea as far as Tamar.*
> *This is the eastern boundary. The southern boundary:*
> *from Tamar to the waters of Meribath-kadesh, thence*
> *to the Wadi of Egypt, and on to the Great Sea. This is*
> *the southern boundary. The western boundary: the*
> *Great Sea forms the boundary up to a point parallel to*
> *Labo of Hamath. This is the western boundary.*

Modern interpretation of the Biblical texts suggests that greater Israel practically covers the territory of the State of Israel and the Palestinian territories. If strict interpretation of the texts is to be applied, the greater Israel concept will cover the modern State of Jordan, some parts of Syria, Egypt, Iraq, Saudi Arabia and Turkey.

The group behind the controversial ideology of greater Israel is the Israeli political party, Likud. **Named "Greater Israel Movement" (Hatnuah Lema'an Eretz Yisrael Hasleimah, in Hebrew)**, the

Likud Party aspired that Israel should "expand" and recover the historic land of Israel. The idea was born in 1977 when Likud Party, led by Menachem Begin (b. 1913 – d. 1992), won for the first time in the Israeli elections, overthrowing the Labor Party. When Likud Party came to power, Begin started to mention in his speeches his loyalty to what he called Judea and Samaria (the West Bank) and went to emphasize that he will transform the area into a Jewish settlement. Begin, however, failed to annex the Gaza Strip and West Bank due to the fact that "absorbing the Palestinians could turn Israel into a binational state instead of a Jewish one."

The **Movement for Greater Israel** was a political organization in the 1960s and 1970s that spearheaded the concept of Greater Israel. However, they garnered very little support from within. Later, they joined the Likud party.

Although some political parties still exist who favor the creation of Greater Israel, the movement has not gathered any support. One reason may be that Israel is still struggling with its Arab neighbors over the land that it already has and thus venturing into such a goal would not be considered a step toward peace.

On September 14, 2008, the then-Prime Minister Ehud Olmert told the Israeli cabinet that the vision of Israel holding onto the West Bank and Gaza Strip as part of its sovereign territory was no longer a viable option. He said, "Greater Israel is over. There is no such thing. Anyone who talks that way is deluding themselves."[48]

---

[48] "Olmert: There's no such thing as 'Greater Israel' anymore" – Haaretz.com

11. Judaism's Holy Sites in Jerusalem

Jews trace their spiritual and historical connection to Jerusalem to as early as the 10th century BC during the building of the Temple of Solomon. For over three thousand years, Jerusalem is the ancestral and spiritual homeland of the Jewish people.

All over Jerusalem and the entire area of Palestine, a number of Jewish religious sites are seen and maintained until today. Among the more popular Jewish sites in Jerusalem are the City of David, the Temple Mount (Al-Aqsa for Muslims), the Tombs of the Prophets, Zedekiah's Cave, the Tomb of Habakkuk, the Massada, Samson's Tomb, Hurva Synagogue, Tombs of the Patriarchs, and others.

The prominent holy sites for Jews are discussed below.

a. *Temple Mount and Solomon's Temple*

As mentioned earlier, Temple Mount (referred to as the Al-Aqsa or Haram Al-Sharif by Muslims) is one of the most contested religious sites in the world. For Jews, it is one of the most sacred sites. Jewish Law dictates that during prayers, Jews should face **mizrach** toward Jerusalem, and the Temple as all of God's bounty and blessing emanates from that spot. In Judaism, mizrach is the direction that most Jews in the diaspora face during prayer, as

Jewish law states that Jews face the site of the Temple in Jerusalem during prayer.

Solomon's temple was built on Temple Mount (the Al-Aqsa site or referred to as **Haram Al-Sharif** or Noble Sanctuary). Jews also refer to that site as Mount Moriah. Before explaining that any further, it is important to recognize that although the temple of Solomon has a considerable place in Jewish history and religion, and whereas both Solomon and David are recognized by Muslims and Jews due to their mention in Jewish and Islamic scriptures, Muslims don't recognize the temple to ever have existed or it being a place of worship. This is because of the Prophet Muhammad's saying (mentioned earlier) that stated that the first house of worship that was built was the mosque in Makkah followed by the mosque at Al-Aqsa forty years later.

Jews believe that at the Al-Aqsa site (Temple Mount) Abraham had built an altar on which he prepared to sacrifice his son Isaac. Although the majority of Muslims believe that Abraham had prepared to sacrifice his son Ishmael (Ismail) instead, there is no indication that the site was in Jerusalem. Jews also believe that at this site, Jacob (son of Isaac) gathered that stone at which his father Isaac was going to be sacrificed and used that stone as a pillow for one night. Upon waking from that sleep in which he had a dream, Jacob applied some oil that he had received from heaven after which the stone sank deep into the earth thus becoming the **Foundation Stone** on which the sacred Jewish Temple would be built by Solomon. This hallowed site is known as **Bethel**, meaning "Gate or House of Heaven."

Like Muslims, Jews too face in a certain direction when praying. The Talmud records the following on this topic:

> *"A blind man, or one who cannot orient himself, should direct his heart toward his Father in Heaven, as it is said, "They shall pray to the Lord" (Kings I 8). One who stands in the diaspora should face the Land of Israel, as it is said, "They shall pray to You by way of their Land" (ibid). One who stands in the Land of Israel should face Jerusalem, as it is said, "They shall pray to the Lord by way of the city" (ibid). One who stands in Jerusalem should face the Temple ... One who stands in the Temple should face the Holy of Holies ... One who stands in the Holy of Holies should face the Cover of the Ark ... It is therefore found that the entire nation of Israel directs their prayers toward a single location."*

The temple in Jerusalem is associated with many stories that can be found in Islamic and Jewish texts. One of them is that of the building of a calf when Moses spent 40 nights visiting God to receive divine revelation.

According to Jewish texts, **Jeroboam I**, the first king of Israel (around 10th century BC), is known to have introduced a golden calf in the Jerusalem temples. Although Jeroboam is not mentioned in the Quran, both Judaism and Islam refer to the calf in their scriptures. However, both have different versions of the story. The Biblical version of the story is reflected by the following verse:

> *Then Aaron took the gold, melted it down, and molded it into the shape of a calf. When the people saw it, they*

exclaimed, "O Israel, these are the gods who brought you out of the land of Egypt!" (Exodus 32:4)

Quran, on the other hand, shows that Aaron didn't build the calf. Instead, Aaron, being a prophet, discouraged the making of the calf while Moses was away for forty nights receiving commandments from Allah. The following Quranic verses tell that story:

And when Musa (Moses) returned to his people, angry and grieved, he said: "What an evil thing is that which you have done (i.e. worshipping the calf) during my absence. Did you hasten and go ahead as regards the matter of your Lord (you left His worship)?" And he threw down the Tablets and seized his brother by (the hair of) his head and dragged him toward him. Harun (Aaron) said: "O son of my mother! Indeed the people judged me weak and were about to kill me, so make not the enemies rejoice over me, nor put me amongst the people who are Zalimun (wrong-doers)" (Quran 7:150).

And when the anger of Musa (Moses) was calmed down, he took up the tablets; and in their inscription was guidance and mercy for those who fear their Lord (Quran 7:154).

And (remember) when We appointed for Musa (Moses) forty nights, and (in his absence) you took the calf (for worship), and you were Zalimun (wrong-doers) (Quran 2: 51).

The people of the Scripture (Jews) ask you to cause a book to descend upon them from heaven. Indeed they asked Musa (Moses) for even greater than that, when they said: "Show us Allah in public," but they were struck with thunderclap and lightning for their wickedness. Then they worshipped the calf even after clear proofs, evidence, and signs had come to them. (Even) so We forgave them. And We gave Musa (Moses) a clear proof of authority (Quran 4:153).

And the people of Musa (Moses) made in his absence, out of their ornaments, the image of a calf (for worship). It had a sound (as if it was mooing). Did they not see that it could neither speak to them nor guide them to the way? They took it (for worship) and they were Zalimun (wrong-doers) Quran (7:148).

b. Rebuilding of the temple

Jews believe that their sacred temple was situated on the site that is currently the sites of Al-Aqsa mosque and the Dome of the Rock. Some Jews, therefore, still hope for and believe in the rebuilding of the temple at the same site. However, it being a contested site, that dream may not be easy to realize.

The rebuilding of the third temple is rooted in Judaism and is considered a religious obligation and desire on the part of the **Orthodox**[49] and **Conservative**[50] Jews. Jewish text of Tanakh also calls for its construction. However, the **Reform and Reconstructionist**[51] Judaism doesn't believe in the reconstruction

---

[49] **Orthodox Judaism** is a formulation of Judaism that adheres to a relatively strict interpretation and application of the laws and ethics canonized in the Talmudic texts ("Oral Torah"). Generally, Orthodox Judaism consists of two different streams, the Modern Orthodox and the Ultra Orthodox.

[50] **Conservative Judaism** accepts both traditional rabbinic modes of study and modern scholarship and critical text study when considering Jewish religious texts and a commitment to the authority and practice of Jewish law.

of the temple because they regard the temple and the sacrifices in the temple as a primitive form of ritual which Judaism has evolved out of and should not return to.

For Jews, following the weekday Torah reading there is a prayer to **"restore the House of our lives and to cause the Shekhinah (Divine Presence) to dwell among us."** The Amidah[52] contains prayers that state: *"Return in mercy to Jerusalem your city, and dwell in it as you have promised. Rebuild it soon in our day as an eternal structure, and quickly set up in it the throne of David. Blessed are you, O Lord, who rebuilds Jerusalem."* The Amidah ends with a meditation for the restoration of the Temple – *"And may the grain-offering of Judah and Jerusalem be pleasing, as in former days and ancient times"* (Malachi 3:4). In the prayer, Jews pray for all of the elements that are necessary for the coming of the messiah (mashiach) – *in gathering of the exiles; restoration of the religious courts of justice; an end of wickedness, sin and heresy; reward to the righteous; rebuilding of Jerusalem; restoration of the line of King David; and restoration of Temple service.*

---

[51] **Reconstructionist Judaism** is a modern American-based Jewish movement based on the ideas of Mordecai Kaplan (1881–1983). The movement developed from the late 1920s to 1940s, and views Judaism as a progressively evolving civilization.

[52] Amidah is the central prayer of the Jewish liturgy. Observant Jews recite the Amidah at each of the three prayer services in a typical weekday: morning, afternoon, and evening.

Many Christians also believe in the rebuilding of the temple. This is because they too believe that the building of the Third Temple is a precursor to the Messiah's arrival.

The subject of rebuilding the temple has been discussed within Judaism off and on for many years, especially after the formation of Israel. The goal of such aspirations is to restore its grandeur as Jews believe it had before its destruction in the year 70 CE by the Babylonians. But mainstream Judaism does not contemplate rebuilding it as a practical project, not only because of the risks involved, but simply because Jerusalem remains a contested territory.

Earlier, the area of the Al-Aqsa was agreed to be administered by the Jordanian Waqf ministry and according to mutual agreement, Jewish worships in that area were stopped. After Israel's capture of Jerusalem, a specific notice was posted by the **Chief Rabbinate of Israel**. The notice reads as follows:

NOTICE AND WARNING

Entrance to the area of the Temple Mount is forbidden to everyone by Jewish Law owing to the sacredness of the place.
---The Chief Rabbinate of Israel.

Over the years, Muslims have blamed various Jewish organizations to have continued with excavation works in, around and under the Al-Aqsa mosque area in an effort to uncover archaeological and religious artifacts. Many Muslims fear that the ongoing excavation is endangering the foundations of the Al-Aqsa that could result in the eventual collapse of the Al-Aqsa religious sites thus paving the way for Jews to take the next step to rebuild the temple. In the face of these excavations, they, therefore, consider the current prohibitions of Jews visiting the temple area as irrelevant. Israel's standpoint mostly has been that any work in the area has been transparent and has instead focused on making the area safer for visitors.

The following are some of the events related to the excavations around the Al-Aqsa mosque:

- In 2007, major tensions erupted between Muslims and Jews when Israel started to extend a pedestrian ramp to the Magrabi gate that is essentially an entrance allowing tourists to view the gardens of the Al-Aqsa Mosque and the Dome of the Rock. Amr Moussa said in a statement distributed to the Arab representatives at an emergency League meeting in Cairo in 2007, "There are plans to change the features of the city . . ." The Islamic Action Front, or IAF, which is the committee of Muslim scholars in Jordan's largest political opposition group, said in a statement that they "urge . . . proclaiming jihad (holy war) to liberate Al-Aqsa and save it from destruction and sabotage from Jewish usurpers." Saudi Arabia issued a statement condemning Israeli excavations around Jerusalem's Al-Aqsa Mosque and called the international community to stop the digging. Their statement said, "Israel's actions violate the mosque's sacred nature and risk destroying its religious and Islamic features."[53]

---

[53] http://www.saudiembassy.net/archive/2007/news/page700.aspx

- In 1996, Netanyahu and Jerusalem's mayor Ehud Olmert decided to open an exit in the Arab Quarter for the Western Wall Tunnel, which former Prime Minister Shimon Peres had instructed to be put on hold for the sake of peace. This sparked three days of rioting by Palestinians, resulting in about 80 Israelis and Palestinians being killed.[54]

c. The Western Wall

As described earlier, the Temple of Solomon (the first Temple) was built on top of Temple Mount in the 10th century BC, but in the year 586 BC, it was destroyed by the Babylonians. Under the command of Herod the Great, the Second Temple was then completed in 516 BC. Later, Herod the Great implemented a massive expansion project on Temple Mount, but in the year 70 CE, Herod's Temple was destroyed by the invading Romans. The remains of Herod's Temple formed the perimeter wall known today as the Western Wall.

The Western Wall in Jerusalem, also known as the Wailing Wall or simply Kotel, is not only the holiest Jewish site, but is the remaining symbol of Jewish identity as the descendants of Abraham, Isaac and Jacob. For many years, the Western Wall has become the Jewish pilgrimage site and the holiest spot for Jews. Today, the Western Wall is also a Jewish national symbol where most important ceremonies, both religious and secular, are celebrated at the Plaza.

---

[54] http://en.wikipedia.org/wiki/Benjamin_Netanyahu

Jews gather at the western wall to remember, pray and cry over their history. More specifically, they recite the seventy ninth psalm, which was written at the destruction of Jerusalem. The psalm contains the following verses:

1) O God, the nations are come into thine inheritance;

Thy holy temple have they defiled;

They have laid Jerusalem in heaps.

2) The dead bodies of thy servants have they given to be food unto the birds of the heavens,

The flesh of thy saints unto the beasts of the earth.

3) Their blood have they shed like water round about Jerusalem;

And there was none to bury them.

4) We are become a reproach to our neighbors,

A scoffing and derision to them that are round about us.

5) How long, O Jehovah? wilt thou be angry forever?

Shall thy jealousy burn like fire?

6) Pour out thy wrath upon the nations that know thee not,

And upon the kingdoms that call not upon thy name.

7) For they have devoured Jacob,

And laid waste his habitation.

8) Remember not against us the iniquities of our forefathers:

Let thy tender mercies speedily meet us;

For we are brought very low.

9) Help us, O God of our salvation, for the glory of thy name;

And deliver us, and forgive our sins, for thy name's sake.

10) Wherefore should the nations say, Where is their God?

Let the avenging of the blood of thy servants which is shed

Be known among the nations in our sight.

11) Let the sighing of the prisoner come before thee:

According to the greatness of thy power preserve thou those that are appointed to death;

12) And render unto our neighbors sevenfold into their bosom

Their reproach, wherewith they have reproached thee, O Lord.

13) So we thy people and sheep of thy pasture

Will give thee thanks for ever:

We will show forth thy praise to all generations.

It should be noted that the Western Wall is the only site part of Temple Mount that Jews visit for religious purposes and worship. Jews are not allowed to visit other areas of al-Aqsa for religious purposes. The background for this is that after the 1967 war, Moshe Dayan who was also the Foreign Minister of Israel, negotiated with the local Muslim leaders that the Aqsa site will be administered by Muslims and thus also ordered the removal of Israeli flag from the Temple Mount (Aqsa site). His view was that Jews should look to Temple Mount as a historical site that was tied to Judaism and not a religious site. He had stated: *"We must view the Temple Mount as a historic site relating to past memory."*[55]

Some Palestinian clerics, however, have questioned the holiness of even the Western Wall. One of them was **Sheikh Ekrima Sa'id Sabri**, who was the Grand Mufti of Jerusalem and Palestine from October 1994 to July 1, 2006. In an interview to a German magazine, he reportedly said the following:

> *"There is not a single stone in the Wailing Wall relating to Jewish History. The Jews cannot legitimately claim this wall, neither religiously nor historically. The Committee of the League of Nations recommended in 1930 to allow the Jews to pray there, in order to keep them quiet. But by no means did it acknowledge that the wall belongs to them."*

> —Interviewed by German magazine Die Welt, January 17, 2001.

---

[55] Moshe Dayan –Death and Legacy - http://en.wikipedia.org/wiki/Moshe_dayan

d. The Tomb of King David

The significance of King David in Judaism is very important as it was he who commissioned the construction of the First Temple in the 10th century BC. The Tomb of King David is located within Jerusalem on Mount Zion. In the year 1335 CE, the Franciscan missionaries established a monastery at that location, but as a result of the tensions with the Greek Orthodox Church in 1551 CE, the Franciscan monastery was eventually closed.

e. Mount of Olives

The importance of Mount of Olives in the history of Judaism started at the time of King David when the mountain was mentioned in the second Book of Samuel 15:30:[56] "As David went up the Mount of Olives, he wept without ceasing. His head was covered, and he was walking barefoot . . ." For the Christians, the Mount of Olives is also a significant place because according to Christian beliefs, it was at this place that Jesus wept for Jerusalem. The following are some of the religious reasons associated with Mount of Olives:

---

[56] As David went up the Mount of Olives, he wept without ceasing. His head was covered, and he was walking barefoot. All those who were with him also had their heads covered and were weeping as they went.

- The Bible mentions the "ascent of olives" as the route that David used to flee from his son Absalom (2 Sam. 15:30) and the peak from which he prayed to God (2 Sam. 15:32).

- The Mount of Olives appears in Zechariah's description of the End of Days (Zech. 14:4).

- Rabbinic tradition believes that Divine Presence settled on the Mount of Olives after the Temple was destroyed (Lamentations Rabbah, Petichta 25, etc.)

- Rabbinic tradition also believes this site to be the place of the Resurrection at the End of Days. This is why it is considered a holy burial place for Jews. The Jewish cemetery is located on the southern part of the Mount of Olives, which rises to a height of 832 meters above sea level.

f. Select Talmud References to Jerusalem

The following are some of the specific references to Jerusalem in Jewish religious books:

Ten kabs (measures) of wisdom descended to the world: nine were taken by Palestine and one by the rest of the world. Ten kabs (measures) of beauty descended to the world: nine were taken by Jerusalem and one by the rest of the world (Talmud: Kiddushin 49b).

"One who stands [in prayer] in Eretz Yisrael (the land of Israel) should direct his heart toward Jerusalem, if he was standing in Jerusalem, he should direct his

heart   toward   the   holy   Temple"
(Talmud: Berachot 27a).

Why are there not fruits [delicious like those] of Ginosaur in Jerusalem? So that those who made pilgrimage there would not say "If we only went up [to Jerusalem] to eat the fruits of Ginosaur in Jerusalem, it would have been enough." [as not to denigrate the real purpose of going up there - to visit the House of Hashem   (G-d)]
(Talmud: Pesachim 8b)

A snake or scorpion never bit anyone in Jerusalem and a person never said to his fellow there is not enough room for me to sleep in Jerusalem (Talmud: Yoma 21a).

Rabbi Tzadok sat in fasting for forty years in order that Jerusalem not be destroyed . . .(Talmud : Gittin 56a)

g. *Similarity between Jerusalem Stories in Jewish and Islamic Scriptures*

Jerusalem is considered by Jews to be the center of their worship. Judaism clearly has it that once King David started his rule in Jerusalem, one of the first things that he wanted was to bring the **Ark of the Covenant** to the city and to make the tabernacle in Jerusalem. This, he believed, would make Jerusalem the central place of worship for Jews because this was the place that God had chosen for the ark to dwell. The Ark of the Covenant is a vessel described in the Bible that contains the Tablets of Stone on which the Ten Commandments were inscribed. The Jews believe that the

Ark was created by Moses, and the Israelites carried it during their 40 years of wandering in the desert. Whenever the Israelites camped, the Ark was placed in a special and sacred tent, the Tabernacle.

The Jewish text, 1 Kings 8:9-9 states:

> **There was nothing in the ark save the two tables of stone which Moses put there at Horeb, when the LORD made a covenant with the children of Israel when they came out of the land of Egypt.**

About the 40 years of wandering in the desert, the Quran states that Jews were prohibited from entering the Holy Land during those years. The Quran states:

> **(Allah) said: "Therefore it (this holy land) is forbidden to them for forty years; in distraction they will wander through the land. So be not sorrowful over the people who are the Fasiqun (rebellious and disobedient to Allah)" Quran (5:26).**

Although not in the scope of this book, it is clear that although there are many similarities between Judaism and Islam, Muslims believe that Islam came after Judaism and Christianity because the message of God (Allah) had been changed in the revelations of the Bible and Torah. Prophet Muhammad, therefore, brought the renewed and fresh message of God in the Quran. God (Allah) then took the responsibility of protecting the last message from any further corruption or change by people.

Some of the verses in the Quran related to the above are as follows:

The likeness of those who were entrusted with the (obligation of the) Taurat (Torah) (i.e. to obey its commandments and to practice its laws), but who subsequently failed in those (obligations), is as the likeness of a donkey which carries huge burdens of books (but understands nothing from them). How bad is the example of people who deny the Ayat (proofs, evidence, verses, signs, revelations) of Allah. And Allah guides not the people who are Zalimun (wrong-doers, disbelievers) Quran (62:5).

Those to whom We gave the Scripture (Jews and Christians) recognise him (Muhammad or the Ka'bah at Makkah) as they recognise their sons. But verily, a party of them conceal the truth while they know it - [i.e. the qualities of Muhammad which are written in the Taurat (torah) and the Injeel (Gospel)] Quran (2:146).

And in their footsteps, We sent 'Îsa (Jesus), son of Maryam (Mary), confirming the Taurat (torah) that had come before him, and We gave him the Injeel (Gospel), in which was guidance and light and confirmation of the Taurat (torah) that had come before it, a guidance and an admonition for Al-Muttaqun (the pious) Quran (5:46).

(Remember) when Allah will say (on the Day of Resurrection). "O 'Îsa (Jesus), son of Maryam (Mary)! Remember My Favour to you and to your mother when I supported you with Ruh-ul-Qudus [Jibril (Gabriel)] so that you spoke to the people in the cradle and in maturity; and when I taught you writing, Al-Hikmah (the power of understanding), the Taurat (torah) and the Injeel (Gospel); and when you made out of the clay a figure like that of a bird, by My Permission, and you breathed into it, and it became a bird by My

Permission, and you healed those born blind, and the lepers by My Permission, and when you brought forth the dead by My Permission; and when I restrained the Children of Israel from you (when they resolved to kill you) as you came unto them with clear proofs, and the disbelievers among them said: 'This is nothing but evident magic'" Quran (5:110).

O people of the Scripture! (Jews and Christians): "Why do you disbelieve in the Ayat of Allah, [the Verses about Prophet Muhammad present in the Taurat (torah) and the Injeel (Gospel)] while you (yourselves) bear witness (to their truth)" Quran (3:170).

12. Christianity's Holy Sites in Jerusalem

Jerusalem is considered holy for Christians primarily because Jesus was born and crucified in those areas. They also hold it high because it was where Jesus spent the last days of his ministry, and where the Last Supper, and according to Christian beliefs, the Crucifixion and the Resurrection took place. The following are some of the key sites that Christians consider sacred and in some cases they make pilgrimage to those sites.

a. The Church of the Nativity

The Church of the Nativity is in the city of Bethlehem, which is 6 miles south of Jerusalem. This church is one of the oldest operating churches in the world. For Christians, the site is quite significant as it is believed by Christians to be the birth site of Jesus. The New Testament Gospels of Matthew and Luke identify Bethlehem as the birthplace of Jesus of Nazareth. The church is built over the cave that tradition marks as the birthplace of Jesus of Nazareth. The Roman Catholic Church celebrates Jesus's birth on December 25, while the Greek Orthodox Church celebrates it on January 7. Today, the church is a holy site of pilgrimage for both Catholics and Orthodox Christians all over the world.

The mother of Constantine I, Saint Helena, ordered the construction of the Church of the Nativity in 327 CE and by the year 333 CE, the church was completed. However, in the Samaritan revolt of 529 CE, the entire structure was burnt down. In 565 CE, Emperor **Justinian I** ordered the rebuilding of the church and the basilica[57] remains strong until today. The present church is administered jointly by the Roman Catholic Church, the Greek Orthodox Church, and the Armenian Apostolic authorities.

b. The Church of Mary Magdalene

The Church of Mary Magdalene is a Russian Orthodox Church located on the Mount of Olives, near the Garden of Gethsemane in Jerusalem. The church is dedicated to Mary Magdalene (Miryam of Migdal), who, Christians believed, was a follower of Jesus. According to the sixteenth chapter of the Gospel of Mark (Christian text), Mary Magdalene was the first to see Christ after his resurrection.

9) When Jesus rose early on the first day of the week, he appeared first to Mary Magdalene, out of whom he had driven seven demons.

10) She went and told those who had been with him and who were mourning and weeping.

---

[57] After the Roman Empire became officially Christian, the term "basilica" specifically came to refer to a large and important church that has been given special ceremonial rites by the Pope.

11) When they heard that Jesus was alive and that she had seen him, they did not believe it.

12) Afterward Jesus appeared in a different form to two of them while they were walking in the country.

13) These returned and reported it to the rest; but they did not believe them either.

14) Later Jesus appeared to the Eleven as they were eating; he rebuked them for their lack of faith and their stubborn refusal to believe those who had seen him after he had risen.

She is, therefore, considered a crucial and important disciple of Jesus, and seemingly his primary female associate, along with **Mary of Bethany**, who some believe to have been the same woman.

Dedicated to Mary Magdalene, therefore, the church has a very special role in the Russian national Orthodox Church. In 1886, Russian Czar Alexander III ordered the construction of a church to honor his mother, Empress Maria Alexandrovna of Russia.

c. The Church of the Holy Sepulcher

The present site for the Church of the Holy Sepulcher was originally the location of the **Aelia Capitolina** that was a city built in 135 CE as part of Hadrian's plan of turning Jerusalem into a pagan city.[58] In

---

[58] After Jerusalem was destroyed in 70 CE, emperor Hadrian built the city "Aelia Capitolina" at the site of old Jerusalem, which was completely destroyed to its foundations in the Roman attack.

325 CE, Emperor Constantine I ordered the demolition of the structure and built the Church of the Holy Sepulcher instead after a thorough excavation led to the discovery of the tomb of Jesus and the Cross in turn leading to the belief that the site was Jesus's crucifixion site. The religious significance of the Church of the Holy Sepulcher for Christians is thus quite deep. It is also considered as the place where Jesus was eventually buried. Since the 4th century CE, therefore, the church has been an important pilgrimage destination for Christians. Though the primary custodianship of the church is shared among Eastern Orthodox, Armenian Apostolic and the Roman Catholic Churches, the Greek Orthodox has a greater responsibility over the church. Today the Church of the Holy Sepulcher is the headquarters of the Greek Orthodox Patriarchate of Jerusalem.

d. The Church of the Annunciation

The Church of the Annunciation is located in the town of Nazareth, a town in northern Israel. The church is an important holy site for the Roman Catholic Christians because according to their belief it is the place where the Angel Gabriel announced to Mary (Jesus's mother) that she will conceive a child named Jesus. The Church of the Annunciation (also known as the **Minor Basilica of the Annunciation**) is a relatively modern structure completed fairly recently in 1969, but it had been a Christian pilgrimage destination ever since it was built in the middle of the 4th century. Apart from the Catholic majority, the Church of the Annunciation also attracts pilgrims from other Christian groups, such as the Anglican and the Eastern Orthodox.

e. Beliefs about Jesus's Crucifixion in Jerusalem

Christians believe that Jesus was crucified in Jerusalem. According to the New Testament, Jesus was arrested in **Gethsemane** following the Last Supper with the twelve Apostles. Gethsemane is a garden at the foot of the Mount of Olives in Jerusalem most famous as the place where Jesus and his disciples prayed the night before Jesus's believed crucifixion. After being flogged and mocked by Roman soldiers as the "King of the Jews," he was taken to the place of his believed crucifixion. Once at Golgotha, Jesus (or his look alike according to Islamic teachings) was stripped and nailed to the beam and hung between two convicted thieves.

Gethsemane is also the garden where Christians believe the Virgin Mary was buried and, therefore, the site in Jerusalem became a pilgrimage site for early Christians.

However, in Islam, Muslims don't believe that Jesus was crucified, even though they believe that he was going to be captured for that objective. The Quran states:

> **But Allah raised him ['Îsa (Jesus)] up (with his body and soul) unto Himself (and he is in the heavens). And Allah is Ever All-Powerful, All-Wise (Quran 4:158).**

Ibn Kathir in his interpretation of the Quranic verses provides the following account:

"Allah's Prophet `Isa (Jesus) could not live in any one city for long and he had to travel often with his mother, peace be upon them. Even so, the Jews were not satisfied, and they went to the king of Damascus at that time, a Greek polytheist who worshipped the stars. They told him that there was a man in Bayt Al-Maqdis (Al-Aqsa) misguiding and dividing the people, in Jerusalem and stirring unrest among the king's subjects. The king became angry and wrote to his deputy in Jerusalem to arrest the rebel leader, stop him from causing unrest, crucify him and make him wear a crown of thorns. When the king's deputy in Jerusalem received these orders, he went with some Jews to the house that `Isa (Jesus) was residing in, and he was then with twelve, thirteen or seventeen of his companions. That day was a Friday, in the evening. They surrounded `Isa (Jesus) in the house, and when he felt that they would soon enter the house or that he would sooner or later have to leave it, he said to his companions, "Who volunteers to be made to look like me, for which he will be my companion in Paradise" A young man volunteered, but `Isa (Jesus) thought that he was too young. He asked the question a second and third time, each time the young man volunteering, prompting `Isa (Jesus) to say, "Well then, you will be that man." Allah (God) made the young man look exactly like `Isa (Jesus), while a hole opened in the roof of the house, and `Isa was made to sleep and ascended to heaven while asleep.

f. Christian Eschatology

The word "eschatology" is the study of the end of things, whether the end of an individual life, the end of the age, or the end of the world. Some Christians believe that toward the end of times, the global population will convert to Christianity as a result of evangelization. Jesus will appear at the end of the Millennium to lead his people into the heavenly city, the **New Jerusalem**.

Biblical scripture and other writings in the Jewish and Christian religions, such as Protestantism, Orthodox Christianity, and Orthodox Judaism, expect the literal renewal of Jerusalem to take place at the Temple Mount (the site of Al-Aqsa) in accordance with various Judeo-Christian prophecies. Dispensationalists believe in a certain chronologically successive "dispensations" or periods in history in which God relates to human beings in different ways. As for Jerusalem, Dispensationalists (a Protestant evangelical tradition) believe that God has yet to fulfill His promises related to the nation of Israel, which amongst others, includes a future where Jesus, upon His return, will rule the world from Jerusalem for a thousand years. Dispensationalists also believe in a literal New Jerusalem that will come down out of Heaven, which will be an entirely new city of incredible dimensions.

Other Christian sects, such as various Protestant denominations, Mormonism, modernist branches of Christianity and Reform Judaism, believe that such a renewal may already have taken place, or that it will take place at some other location besides the Temple Mount.

The King James Version of the Bible paints the physical description of the New Jerusalem as a city of magnificence and enormity as follows:

"And he carried me away in the spirit to a great and high mountain, and showed me that great city, the holy Jerusalem, descending out of heaven from God, having the glory of God: and her light was like unto a stone most precious, even like a jasper stone, clear as crystal; and had a wall great and high, and had twelve gates, and at the gates twelve angels, and names written thereon, which are the names of the twelve tribes of the children of Israel: on the east three gates; on the north three gates; on the south three gates; and on the west three gates. And the wall of the city had twelve foundations, and in them the names of the twelve apostles of the Lamb" Revelation 21:10-14.

"And he that talked with me had a golden reed to measure the city, and the gates thereof, and the wall thereof. And the city lieth foursquare, and the length is as large as the breadth: and he measured the city with the reed, twelve thousand furlongs. The length and the breadth and the height of it are equal. And he measured the wall thereof, a hundred and forty and four cubits, according to the measure of a man, that is, of the angel" Revelation 21:15-17.

"And the building of the wall of it was of jasper: and the city was pure gold, like unto clear glass. And the foundations of the wall of the city were garnished with all manner of precious stones. The first foundation was jasper; the second, sapphire; the third, a chalcedony; the fourth, an emerald; The fifth, sardonyx; the sixth, sardius; the seventh, chrysolyte; the eighth, beryl; the ninth, a topaz; the tenth, a chrysoprasus; the eleventh,

a jacinth; the twelfth, an amethyst" Revelation 21:18-20.

Christians also believe that in the New Jerusalem, physical and spiritual life will be illuminated by the presence of the God and thus there won't be any need for the sun, the moon, or the building of a temple. The King James Version of the Bible states:

"And I saw no temple therein: for the Lord God Almighty and the Lamb are the temple of it. And the city had no need of the sun, neither of the moon, to shine in it: for the glory of God did lighten it, and the Lamb is the light thereof" Revelation 21:22-23.

g. Other Christian Sites in Jerusalem

Other than the major Christian pilgrimage and holy sites in Jerusalem, there are many other important sites within Jerusalem, such as the Chapel of the Ascension, the Church of John the Baptist, the Church of Dominus Flevit, the Church of All Nations, the Church of the *Pater Noster*, the Church of the Visitation, the Church of the Holy Redeemer, the Tomb of Lazarus, the Last Supper Room, the Tomb of the Virgin, and the Via Dolorosa, among others.

13. Islam's Holy Sites in Jerusalem

As mentioned earlier, Jerusalem has a special place in Islam as well. There are references about Jerusalem in both Quran (Word of God) and Hadith (Traditions and sayings of Prophet Muhammad). The following provides an overview of the religious significance of Jerusalem in Islam.

a. Al-Aqsa Mosque

"Masjid Al-Aqsa" (translated as the "Farthest Mosque" or "al-Aqsa Mosque") is the third holiest site in Islam after the cities of Makkah and Madinah. The religious significance of Al-Aqsa Mosque in Islamic traditions is rather deep. In fact, the term "Al-Aqsa Mosque" refers not only to the mosque itself, but to the entire area that is called the Temple Mount. Some refer to the entire area of Temple Mount as "Al-Aqsa" or the "Al-Aqsa Site" or "Haram Al-Sharif" and the mosque at the site as "Al-Aqsa Mosque".

Masjid al-Aqsa was the first of the two qiblahs (direction of prayers), and is one of the three mosques to which people may specifically travel for the purpose of worship. As stated in Prophet Muhammad's Hadith book, Sunan al-Nasaa'i (693), it was built by Solomon (Prophet Suleiman).

Al-Aqsa mosque was first expanded and rebuilt by Umayyad Caliph Abd al-Malik. The entire Al-Aqsa Mosque was fully completed by the son of Caliph Abd al-Malik, al Walid, in 705 CE. Like the Dome of the Rock, the Al-Aqsa Mosque suffered the same fate when earthquake hit Jerusalem in 746 A.D, but it was immediately rebuilt in 754 CE.

The ownership of al-Aqsa has been one of the contentious issues in the Israel-Palestinian conflict. Israel claims sovereignty over the mosque along with all of the Temple Mount (Al-Aqsa / Haram Al-Sharif), but Palestinians hold unofficial custodianship of the site through the administration of the mosque through an Islamic waqf, which is believed to be an independent body. Palestinians have demanded complete ownership of the mosque and other Islamic holy sites in East Jerusalem. This issue, therefore, still remains to be contentious.

Al-Aqsa holds a spiritual place in the lives of Muslims for the following reasons:

1) Al-Aqsa was the first qiblah (direction of prayers) for Muslims.
2) Prophet Muhammad's famous trip / ascension to the heavens and skies was from the Al-Aqsa site. This site was chosen to be so important that the prophet was first brought to Al-Aqsa from Makkah and then taken from Al-Aqsa to the heavens for a night journey.
3) Islamic teachings have specifically designated Al-Aqsa as the third holiest site in Islam.

4) According to Islamic traditions, Al-Aqsa was the second house of worship built on earth following the mosque in Makkah.

5) The religious significance led to Muslims in history flocking to the city and thus Islamic history became more intertwined with events in Jerusalem, making Al-Aqsa site / Haram Al-Sharif hold an important place in Islamic history.

6) According to the prophesies of Prophet Muhammad, the Holy Land will be the site of significant events toward the end of times, especially when Muslims and the world will go through hard times during the time of the Anti-Christ.

First Qiblah

The historical and religious significance of Al-Aqsa Mosque is emphasized by the fact that the mosque was the first *qibla* (direction) used for praying. The Muslims turned toward al-Aqsa mosque during prayers for a period of sixteen or seventeen months after migration from Makkah to Madina in 642 CE. Later, however, the direction was changed and today all Muslims in the world turn toward Kaaba in Makkah during moments of prayers.

It was after 16 months of Hijrah (migration from Makkah to Medina) that Prophet Muhammad was ordered by Allah to face Makkah when offering prayers. The Quran states:

"Verily, We have seen the turning of your (Muhammad's) face toward the heaven. Surely, We shall turn you to a Qiblah (prayer direction) that shall please you, so turn your face in the direction of Al-Masjid Al-Haraam (at Makkah). And wheresoever you people are, turn your faces (in prayer) in that direction" *[al-Baqraah 2:144].*

Me'raj-Acension to the Skies (Makkah to Jerusalem to the Heavens)

When Prophet Muhammad went on **al-Me'raj** (the night journey ascension to the skies), he was first brought to Al-Aqsa mosque in Jerusalem. The trip from Makkah to Jerusalem is referred to as **al-Isra**. In Jerusalem, the prophet met all the previous messengers of God and led them in prayers in one prayer in al-Aqsa. This is mentioned in a lengthy Hadith by the prophet one of the statements of which is as follows:

"... Then the time for prayer came, and I led them in prayer" (Narrated in the book of Muslim, 172, from the Hadith of Abu Hurayrah).

The fact that Prophet Muhammad went to Me'raj (ascension to the skies) from here is also mentioned in the Quran. This certified an ever living and non-diminishing importance of the Al-Aqsa site in the eyes of the Muslims. The Quran states the following:

"Glorified (and Exalted) be He (Allah), Who took His slave (Muhammad) for a journey by night from Al-

Masjid-al-Haram (at Makkah) to the farthest mosque (in Jerusalem), the neighborhood whereof We have blessed, in order that We might show him (Muhammad) of Our Ayaat (proofs, evidences, lessons, signs, etc.). Verily, He is the All-Hearer, the All-Seer" (Quran: 17:1).

Regarding the event of ascension to the heaven from Jerusalem, Anas ibn Malik quotes Prophet Muhammad in a Hadith quoted in the book of Muslim:

"An animal, al-buraq was brought to me. Although it is an animal smaller in size than a mule yet bigger than a donkey, but still it can place its hoof at a distance equal to the range of vision. When I mounted it, it brought me to Bait-al Maqdis (Jerusalem). First I tethered it in the same ring as used by previous prophets then entered the Mosque to offer two rak'at (of prayers) there. When I came out Gabriel brought me two utensils. One contained wine while the other contained milk, I chose milk over wine. Seeing this, Gabriel said, 'You have chosen al-fitra (the natural way).'

Gabriel then accompanied me into the lower heavens and requested them to open. We heard a voice that said "Who are you?" and he responded "Gabriel". Then the same voice asked "Who is with you?" and Gabriel responded "Muhammad". The voice asked "Has revelation been sent to him?" and Gabriel said "Revelation has been sent to him." Upon hearing this, the gates opened and I met Adam. Adam welcomed me and prayed for my well-being.

Gabriel then accompanied me into the second heaven and requested them to open. We heard a voice that said "Who are you?" and he responded "Gabriel". Then the same voice asked "Who is with you?" and Gabriel responded "Muhammad". The voice asked "Has revelation been sent to him?" and Gabriel said "Revelation has been sent to him." Upon hearing this, the gates opened and I met Jesus and John. They welcomed me and prayed for my well-being.

Gabriel then accompanied me into the third heaven and requested them to open. We heard a voice that said "Who are you?" and he responded "Gabriel". Then the same voice asked "Who is with you?" and Gabriel responded "Muhammad". The voice asked "Has revelation been sent to him?" and Gabriel said "Revelation has been sent to him." Upon hearing this, the gates opened and I met Joseph, who was given a great portion of beauty. Joseph welcomed me and prayed for my well-being.

Gabriel then accompanied me into the fourth heaven and requested them to open. We heard a voice that said "Who are you?" and he responded "Gabriel". Then the same voice asked "Who is with you?" and Gabriel responded "Muhammad". The voice asked "Has revelation been sent to him?" and Gabriel said "Revelation has been sent to him." Upon hearing this, the gates opened and I met Enoch (Younus). Enoch welcomed me and prayed for my well-being.

Gabriel then accompanied me into the fifth heaven and requested them to open. We heard a voice that said "Who are you?" and he responded "Gabriel". Then the same voice asked "Who is with you?" and Gabriel responded "Muhammad". The voice asked "Has revelation been sent to him?" and Gabriel said "Revelation has been sent to him." When the gates opened I met Aaron (Harun). He welcomed me and prayed for my well-being.

Gabriel then accompanied me into the sixth heaven and requested them to open. We heard a voice that said "Who are you?" and he responded "Gabriel". Then the same voice asked "Who is with you?" and Gabriel responded "Muhammad". The voice asked "Has revelation been sent to him?" and Gabriel said "Revelation has been sent to him." When the gates opened I met Moses (Moosa). He welcomed me and prayed for my well-being.

Gabriel then accompanied me into the seventh heaven and requested them to open. We heard a voice that said "Who are you?" and he responded "Gabriel". Then the same voice asked "Who is with you?" and Gabriel responded "Muhammad". The voice asked "Has revelation been sent to him?" and Gabriel said "Revelation has been sent to him." When the gates opened I met Abraham (Ibraheem). Abraham was leaning against the bayt al-ma`mur. Bayt al-ma`mur is a place where seventy thousand angels enter every day to never return.

Next I was brought to the sidrat al-muntaha, the Lote Tree of the Furthest Limit. The sidrat al-muntaha has leaves like the ears of an elephant and fruit that seems insignificant at first. But at the command of Allah the fruit of this tree transforms into such beauty that no one in creation can find words to describe it. Then Allah revealed what He revealed to me. He made fifty prayers compulsory for me every night and day.

I started descending and reached Moses. Moses asked me: 'What has your Lord made obligatory for your community?' I told him, 'Fifty prayers'. He responded, 'Return to your Lord and ask Him to reduce them, your community will not be able to bear that. I know the people of Israel from long experience and I have tested them.' Hearing this I returned to my Lord and requested, 'O Lord, make things lighter for my people.' My Lord reduced it by five prayers. I returned to Moses who asked the same question, and then he said 'Your community will not be able to stand that. So return and ask Him to make things lighter.' I kept going between my Lord and Moses until He said, "O Muhammad, there are five prayers every night and day. Each prayer is equal to ten prayers making them equal to fifty prayers. Whoever intends a good deed and does not do it, there will be written for him a single good deed. If he does it then there will be written for him ten good deeds. Whoever intends an evil deed and does not do it then there is nothing written against him. If he does it then there is written for him one evil deed.'

I once again started my descent and reached Moses. He asked me the same question and I responded. He said, 'Return to your Lord and ask Him to make things lighter.' Muhammad, peace be upon him, said, 'I have returned to my Lord until I felt ashamed before Him."

In Islam, this was considered a miracle bestowed on Prophet Muhammad by God that in one night the Prophet was taken from Makkah to Al-Aqsa mosque in Jerusalem, where he met all the previous prophets. He conducted the prayers and led all of them in prayers. From the Farthest Mosque, Al-Aqsa, the Prophet was then taken to the skies, where he met God (Allah), was shown His signs and got religious guidance that includes the compulsory five prayers that Muslims pray daily.

This very event played an important role in further strengthening the spiritual and emotional ties of the Muslims with Jerusalem. That, in addition to the many references of Jerusalem in the Quran, has made Muslims hold Jerusalem very close to their hearts.

Third Most Sacred Site for Muslims

Many quotes of Prophet Muhammad clearly establish the importance of the mosque. According to a famous Hadith by Prophet Mohammad:

"A prayer in the Sacred Mosque (in Makkah) is worth 100,000 prayers, a prayer in my mosque (in Medina) is worth 1000 and a prayer in Jerusalem is worth 250 prayers more than in any other mosque."

This Hadith clearly established Al-Aqsa mosque as the third holiest site for Muslims. Another Hadith to support this is the following where he said:

"No journeys should be made specifically to visit any mosque except three: al-Masjid al-Haraam [in Makkah], this mosque of mine [in Madinah] and al-Masjid al-Aqsa [in al-Quds/Jerusalem]." (Saheeh Books – agreed upon by the famous Hadith scholars).

Another Hadith states the following:

It was reported that Abu Dharr said: we were discussing, in the presence of the Prophet (peace be upon him), which of them was more virtuous, the mosque of the Messenger of Allah or Bayt al-Maqdis (in Jerusalem). The Messenger of Allah said: One prayer in my mosque is better than four prayers there, but it is still a good place of prayer. Soon, there will come a time when if a man has a spot of land as big as his horse's rope from which he can see Bayt al-Maqdis, that will be better for him than the whole world. (Narrated and classed as saheeh by al-Haakim, 4/509. Al-Dhahabi and al-Albaani agreed with him, as stated in al-Silsilah al-Saheehah, at the end of the discussion of Hadith no. 2902).

Second House of Worship on Earth

According to Islamic teachings, Masjid Al-Aqsa was the second house of worship established on earth. According to one of the hadiths:

It was stated by Abu Dharr: "I said, 'O Messenger of Allah, which mosque was built on earth first?' He said, 'Al-Masjid al-Haraam [in Makkah].' I said, 'Then which?' He said, 'Al-Masjid al-Aqsa.' I said, 'How much time was there between them?' He said, 'Forty years. So wherever you are when the time for prayer comes, pray, for that is the best thing to do.'" [Narrated in the book of al-Bukhaari, 3366; Muslim, 520.]

Spiritual Connection

Jerusalem is known to have been the seat of other prophets as well. In Islam, Prophet Yahya (John the Baptist) was Jesus's contemporary and preached in Jerusalem. The following is an account of Yahya's preaching stated in Ibn Kathir's interpretation and as stated in a Hadith by the Prophet:

"Allah commanded Yahya bin Zakariya (John son of Zacharaiyyah) to implement five commands and to order the Children of Israel to implement them, but Yahya was slow in carrying out these commands. 'Isa (Jesus) said to Yahya, `You were ordered to implement

*five commands and to order the Children of Israel to
implement them. So either order, or I will do it.' Yahya
said, 'My brother! I fear that if you do it before me, I will
be punished or the earth will be shaken under my feet.'
Hence, Yahya bin Zakariya called the Children of Israel
to Bayt Al-Maqdis (Jerusalem), until they filled the
Masjid (mosque). He sat on the balcony, thanked Allah
and praised him and then said, `Allah ordered me to
implement five commandments and that I should order
you to adhere to them. The first is that you worship
Allah alone and not associate any with Him (in worship
as God). The example of this command is the example
of a man who bought a servant from his money with
paper or gold. The servant started to work for the
master, but was paying the profits to another person.
Who among you would like his servant to do that Allah
created you and sustains you? Therefore, worship Him
alone and do not associate anything with Him. I also
command you to pray, for Allah directs His Face
toward His servant's face, as long as the servant does
not turn away. So when you pray, do not turn your
heads to and fro. I also command you to fast. The
example of it is the example of a man in a group of
men and he has some musk wrapped in a piece of
cloth, and consequently, all of the group smells the
scent of the wrapped musk. Verily, the odor of the
mouth of a fasting person is better before Allah than
the scent of musk. I also command you to give charity.
The example of this is the example of a man who was
captured by the enemy. They tied his hands to his neck
and brought him forth to cut off his neck. He said to
them, 'Can I pay a ransom for myself?' He kept
ransoming himself with small and large amounts until
he liberated himself. I also command you to always
remember Allah. The example of this deed is that of a
man who the enemy is tirelessly pursuing. He takes
refuge in a fortified fort. When the servant remembers
Allah, he will be resorting to the best refuge from
Satan.)"*

The Quran also states:

"O my people! Enter the holy land (Palestine) which Allah has assigned to you, and turn not back (in flight) for then you will be returned as losers" [al-Maa'idah 5:21].

Jerusalem has been associated with many prophets. Islam considers itself a continuation of the message that was brought by the previous prophets, some of whom were Moses, David, Solomon, and Jesus because they all preached the Sovereignty of God. Therefore, it is but natural that Jerusalem is held sacred by the Muslims, due to the city's connection to these prophets. The Quran mentions the names of a number of prophets who were sent by God.

Jerusalem is also the final resting place for some of the noblest people on earth including prophets. Although not confirmed, many believe that the graves of Abraham, Ishaq (Isaac) and Yaqub (Jacob) are in Jerusalem. According to some accounts, more than 100 prophets are buried in Jerusalem. All these prophets are highly revered and respected in Islam.

The Death of Anti-Christ

Al-Aqsa mosque is considered so sacred in Islam that according to Islamic texts, the one-eyed Dajjaal ("Antichrist") will not be able to enter it. This is mentioned in the following Hadith:

"He will prevail over all the earth, apart from al-Haram [in Makkah] and Bayt al-Maqdis (in Jerusalem)." (Narrated as Hadith by Ahmad, 19665. Classed as saheeh by Ibn Khuzaymah, 2/327, and Ibn Hibbaan, 7/102.)

According to Islamic scriptures, the Dajjaal (anti-Christ) will be killed close to al-Quds in Jerusalem in a place called Ludd. He will be killed by the Messiah (Jesus) 'Eesa ibn Maryam (peace be upon him), as was stated in the Hadith:

"The son of Maryam will kill the Dajjaal at the gates of Ludd" (Hadith by Sahih Muslim, 2937).

Ludd (Lod) is a city near the Al-Aqsa and is located about 15 kilometers (9 miles) southeast of Tel Aviv in the Center District of Israel. Israel's main international airport, Ben Gurion International Airport (previously called Lydda Airport, and Lod Airport) is located in the city.

b. The Dome of the Rock

The Dome of the Rock was constructed under the leadership of Umayyad Caliph Abd al-Malik ibn Marwan who commissioned two engineers to take charge of the project: Yazid Ibn Salam, who was from Jerusalem, and Raja Ibn Haywah, from Baysan. Built between 689 CE and 691 CE, the Dome of the Rock (Masjid As-Sakhrah) is one of the oldest Islamic buildings in the world. This structure was built to commemorate the event of the Al-Israa and AL-Me'raj (Ascension to the heavens). It is built on top of the Al-Qasa site (Temple Mount) in Jerusalem referred to as the "Sacred Noble Sanctuary" or al-Haram ash-Sharif. The religious significance of the site is derived from the fact that the Dome of the Rock has the rock at the center of the dome, where Prophet Muhammad ascended into heaven accompanied by the angel Gabriel.

The Dome of the Rock is situated in the middle of the plateau of al-Masjid al-Aqsa (Temple Mount), which is in the southeastern part of the city of al-Quds (Jerusalem). The plateau measures 480 meters from north to south, and 300 meters from east to west and occupies approximately one-fifth of the area of the Old City of Jerusalem.

Some mistakenly take the Dome of the Rock as the Al-Aqsa mosque. However, because the pictures of the Dome are so widespread (because of its architecture), many think of it as the mosque, whereas the Mosque is situated in the southern portion of the plateau, and the Dome is built on the raised rock that is situated in the middle of the plateau.

Although the Dome of the Rock is a rich source of Islamic inspiration in the holy city of Jerusalem (due to the reasons explained earlier), there are no religious rituals associated with this site. Ibn Taymiyah (one of the very renowned Islamic scholars) states the following in his book *Majmoo'at al-Rasaa'il al-Kubra, 2/61:*

> **"With regard to the Rock, neither 'Umar nor any of the Sahaabah (companions of the Prophet) prayed there, and there was no dome over it during the time of the**

Rightly-Guided Caliphs. It was open to the sky during the caliphate of 'Umar, 'Uthmaan, 'Ali, Mu'aawiyah, Yazeed and Marwaan... The scholars among the Sahaabah and those who followed them in truth did not venerate the rock because it was an abrogated qiblah... rather it was venerated by the Jews and some of the Christians."

c. Quranic and Other Islamic References to Jerusalem

Although the word "Jerusalem" doesn't explicitly appear in the Quran, there are numerous references to the city both in the Quran and Hadith (Prophetic sayings). The following are some of those references from the Quran. The word "Jerusalem" mentioned in the verses in parentheses is the interpretation and the indirect reference to Jerusalem.

And We divided them into twelve tribes (as distinct) nations. We directed Moosa (Moses) by inspiration, when his people asked him for water, (saying): "Strike the stone with your stick", and there gushed forth out of it twelve springs: each group knew its own place for water. We shaded them with the clouds and sent down upon them Al-Manna and the quails (saying): "Eat of the good things with which We have provided you." They harmed Us not but they used to harm themselves (Quran: 7: 160).

And (remember) when it was said to them: "Dwell in this town (Jerusalem) and eat there from wherever you wish, and say, (O Allah) forgive our sins; and enter the gate prostrate (bowing with humility). We shall forgive you your wrong-doings. We shall increase (the reward) for the good-doers" (Quran: 7: 161).

And (remember) when We said: "Enter this town (Jerusalem) and eat bountifully therein with pleasure and delight wherever you wish, and enter the gate in prostration (or bowing with humility) and say: Forgive us, and We shall forgive you your sins and shall increase (reward) for the good-doers" (Quran: 2:158).

And (remember) when Moosa (Moses) said to his people: "O my people! Remember the Favor of Allah to you, when He made Prophets among you, made you kings, and gave you what He had not given to any other among the Alameen (mankind and jinns, in the past) " (Quran: 5: 20).

"O my people! Enter the holy land (Palestine) which Allah has assigned to you, and turn not back (in flight) for then you will be returned as losers" (Quran: 5: 21).

"Narrated Jabir bin Abdullah who heard Allah's Apostle saying: When the people of Quraish did not believe me (i.e. the story of my Night Journey), I stood up in al-Hijr and Allah displayed Jerusalem in front of me, and I began describing it to them while I was looking at it" (Sahih Bukhari).

"Narrated Maimunah ibn Sa'ad: I said: Apostle of Allah, tell us the legal injunction about (visiting) Bait al-Muqaddas (Jerusalem). The Apostle of Allah said: Go and pray there. (But) all the cities at that time were affected by war. (So he added) If you cannot visit it and pray there, then send some oil to be used in the lamps (i.e. send support)" (Hadith Book of Sunan Abu Dawud).

They said: "O Moosa (Moses)! We shall never enter it as long as they are there. So go you and your Lord and fight you two, we are sitting right here" Quran (5:24).

He (Moosa (Moses)) said: "O my Lord! I have power only over myself and my brother, so separate us from the people who are the Fasiqoon (rebellious and disobedient to Allah)!" Quran (5:25)

(Allah) said: "Therefore it (this holy land) is forbidden to them for forty years; in distraction they will wander through the land. So be not sorrowful over the people who are the Fasiqoon (rebellious and disobedient to Allah) " Quran (5:26).

(26) Narrated Abu Huraira: On the night Allah's Apostle was taken on a night journey (Me'raj) two cups, one containing wine and the other milk, were presented to him at Jerusalem. He looked at it and took the cup of milk. Gabriel said, "Praise be to Allah Who guided you to Al-Fitra (the right path); if you had taken (the cup of) wine, your nation would have gone astray" (Book #69, Hadith #482) Bukhari.

Narrated Maymunah ibn Sa'd: I said: Apostle of Allah, tell us the legal injunction about (visiting) Bayt al-Muqaddas (the dome of the Rock at jerusalem). The Apostle of Allah (peace_be_upon_him) said: go and pray there. All the cities at that time were affected by war. If you cannot visit it and pray there, then send some oil to be used in the lamps (Book #2, Hadith #0457) AbuDawood.

"So her Lord (Allah) accepted her with goodly acceptance. He made her grow in a good manner and put her under the care of Zakariya (Zachariya). Every time he entered Al-Mihrab to (visit) her, he found her (Maryam) supplied with sustenance. He said: "O Maryam (Mary)! From where have you got this?" She said, "This is from Allah." Verily, Allah provides sustenance to whom He wills, without limit" (Quran: 3:37).

Then the angels called him, while he was standing in prayer in Al-Mihrab (a praying place or a private room), (saying): "Allah gives you glad tidings of Yahya (John), confirming (believing in) the Word from Allah (i.e. the creation of Iesa (Jesus), the Word from Allah ("Be!" - and he was!)), noble, keeping away from sexual relations with women, a Prophet, from among the righteous" (Quran: 3:39).

"Then he (Zakariya) came out to his people from Al-Mihrab (a praying place or a private room, etc.), he told them by signs to glorify Allah's Praises in the morning and in the afternoon (Quran: 19:11).

14. The United States' Stance on Jerusalem

Although the United States has many strong allies in the Middle East, Israel enjoys the status of a close and special ally. This is reflected in the substantial yearly foreign aid that Israel receives from the United States. As stated earlier, this aid averages about $3 Billon per year and is in the form of economic and military grants, refugee settlement assistance, and other aids.

It is, therefore, no secret that the United States is the strongest supporter of Israel as the Jewish homeland in Palestine. In fact, the relationship of Israel and the United States started within minutes after Israel declared its independence on May 15, 1948, when President Harry Truman recognized Israel as an independent country. All through the history of Israel, the United States government along with various civic groups, labor unions, political parties, and members of the American and world Jewish communities expressed support to the Balfour Declaration that stipulated the creation of a Jewish homeland.

The overwhelming support of the US government and the support for some particular factions within the US has led US to always play a dominant and leading role in the peace-keeping of the Middle East. There were, however, frictions in the past when the United States transferred arms to its allies in the Middle East for purposes of individual and collective defenses. The arms transfers to Arab countries were seen by Israel as a real threat against its national security and peace.

The position of Jerusalem as the capital of Israel has been quite controversial. Although Israel's declared capital is Jerusalem, this is not internationally recognized due to Jerusalem being the spiritual center for the world's major religions and Arabs and Muslims keeping the utmost pressure on the United States, United Nations, and other countries. Therefore, most countries have been reluctant to support the recognition of Jerusalem as Israel's capital. This is the reason why most embassies have been located elsewhere in Israel. The US's stance on this matter, however, has been mostly in favor of recognizing Jerusalem as Israel's capital and thus it supports the moving of the US Embassy from Tel Aviv to Jerusalem. In support of that, an act was specifically passed in 1995 by the US Congress to facilitate the move of the US embassy to Jerusalem. The proposed law was adopted by the Senate with a voting tally of 93-5, and the House passed it with a vote of 374-37. A section of the law states the following:

SEC. 3. TIMETABLE.

(a) STATEMENT OF THE POLICY OF THE UNITED STATES:

(1) Jerusalem should remain an undivided city in which the rights of every ethnic and religious group are protected.

(2) Jerusalem should be recognized as the capital of the State of Israel; and

(3) The United States Embassy in Israel should be established in Jerusalem no later than May 31, 1999.

(b) OPENING DETERMINATION:

Not more than 50 per cent of the funds appropriated to the Department of State for fiscal year 1999 for "Acquisition and Maintenance of Buildings Abroad" may be obligated until the Secretary of State determines and reports to Congress that the United States Embassy In Jerusalem has officially opened.

This law was passed for the purposes of initiating and funding the relocation of the United States Embassy in Israel from Tel Aviv to Jerusalem, no later than May 31, 1999. As is clear, the law attempted to withhold 50 percent of the funds appropriated to the State Department specifically for "Acquisition and Maintenance of Buildings Abroad" until the United States Embassy in Jerusalem had officially opened.

Though the law was passed, it has never been implemented because of the opposition from certain presidents including Clinton, George W. Bush, and Barack Obama. They have viewed this matter as a Congressional infringement on the Executive Branch's constitutional authority over foreign policy; and thus have consistently claimed the presidential waiver on national security interests.

15. Israeli-Arab Relations

Although Israel is a small country geographically, its military strength is one of the world's strongest and highly developed. The influence and support of the United States has helped Israel achieve that status. Therefore, even with a short history as a country, Israel has been able to successfully fight many wars against most of its Arab neighbors—from Lebanon to the north, Jordan to the east, Egypt to the south and many other Arab nations as far as Iraq who conspired against Israel.

On the same token, the United States has also played an instrumental role in peace negotiations between Arabs and Israel for many decades. This has resulted in a series of peace treaties and accords. The following are some of the most important peace accords Israel has had with the Arabs.

a. Camp David Accords

In this peace treaty, the United States witnessed the initiatives of Israel and Egypt to come up with a peaceful resolution regarding their respective disputes. After twelve days of secret negotiations at Camp David, the peace treaty was signed by Egyptian President Anwar El Sadat and Israeli Prime Minister Menachem Begin and witnessed by United States President Jimmy Carter on September 17, 1978, at the White House.

As a result of the peace treaty, Israel and Egypt laid out three important agreements.

a) To establish an autonomous or self-governing authority in the West Bank and the Gaza Strip.

b) To withdraw Israeli armed forces from Sinai and return Sinai to Egypt.

c) Unites States was to give both Israel and Egypt annual subsidies.

b. Oslo Accords

In this peace treaty between Israel and the Palestinian Liberation Organization (PLO), United States President Bill Clinton witnessed the first ever direct, face-to-face agreement between Israeli Prime Minister Yitzhak Rabin and PLO Chairman Yasser Arafat. After a series of negotiations in Oslo, Norway, that started as early as 1991, the documents were signed on September 13, 1993, in Washington, DC, by Mahmoud Abbas, representing the Palestinian Liberation Organization, Foreign Minister Shimon Peres, representing Israel, Secretary of State Warren Christopher of the United States and Foreign Minister Andrei Kozyrev of Russia.

At the Oslo Accords, Israel and the Palestinian Liberation Organization agreed to implement the following important agreements:

a) The creation of a Palestinian National Authority (PNA).

b) The withdrawal of Israeli armed forces from West Bank and the Gaza Strip.

Back in Israel, the Oslo Accords triggered a strong debate in the Knesset on whether or not the agreements set forth in the treaty were reasonable. The left leaning members of the Israeli political parties issued a unanimous support for the treaty, while the right wing members of the Knesset issued an opposition. After much discussion, a voting was held and 61 Knesset members favored the agreement, while 54 Knesset members voted against the agreement.

c. Israel-Jordan Peace Treaty

Once again in 1994, United States President Bill Clinton witnessed another signing of a peace treaty, this time between Israel and its eastern neighbor, Jordan. The peace treaty was signed at the southern border crossing of Aravah (the border that separates Israel and Jordan) on October 26, 1994, by Israeli Prime Minister Yitzhak Rabin and Jordanian Prime Minister Abdul Salam Majali.

The primary objective of the peace treaty was to resolve territorial disputes between Israel and Jordan, but other important principles were also agreed:

a) The Israeli-Jordanian border is to be set at the Jordan River.
b) There is to be full normalization between Israel and Jordan, including the establishment of diplomatic relations, the opening of embassies, granting of tourist visas, opening a flight connection, access to seaports and establishment of free trade zones and industrial parks.
c) The recognition and respect for the sovereignty and territory of each side.

d. Geneva Accord

The sole objective of The Draft Permanent Status Agreement, otherwise known as the Geneva Accord or Geneva Initiative, is meant to end the long-standing Israeli-Palestinian conflict. The agreement was initiated in 2002 by **Alexis Keller** and officially launched on December 1, 2003. The agreement was created by Israeli politician **Yossi Beilin** and former Palestinian Authority minster **Yasser Abed Rabbo.**

The thrust of the agreement was to establish a Palestinian state on the West Bank and the Gaza Strip and in return the newly created Palestinian state will recognize the state of Israel as the rightful homeland of the Jewish people. The creators of the Geneva Accord believed that reaching this kind of agreement will solve the Israeli-

Palestinian conflict. But the government of Israel immediately rejected the proposal, while Palestinian Authority never really got interested in the agreement. In the United States, former president Jimmy Carter endorsed the accord along with former Joint Chiefs of Staff General Colin Powell.

16. Current Arab Resistance – PLO vs HAMAS

The Palestinian Liberation Organization (PLO) and HAMAS (Harakat al-Muqawamat al-Islamiyya, which means Islamic Resistance Movement) have almost identical political aspirations for Palestine in that they both aspire for the liberation of the Palestinian people from Israel who they believe is occupying their land. The difference, however, in both their aspirations is the underlying ideology in achieving these political aspirations.

The PLO was organized as a political party in 1964 by the Arab League (which consists of Egypt, Iraq, Jordan, Lebanon, Saudi Arabia, Syria and Yemen) to represent the Palestinian people. This representation is recognized by more than a hundred states around the world when the State of Palestine declared its independence on November 15, 1988, in which it now maintains diplomatic relations. PLO was the major player behind the declaration of independence. Since 1974, the State of Palestine has enjoyed observer status at the United Nations. Today, the PLO is headed by Mahmoud Abbas, the President of the Palestinian National Authority.

As a legitimate political organization, the PLO laid out its Ten Point Program on June 9, 1974, during the 12th Palestine National Council:[59]

---

[59] Political Programme of the 12th Palestine National Council - http://en.wikisource.org/wiki/Political_Programme_of_the_12th_Palestine_National_Council

1. To reaffirm the Palestine Liberation Organization's previous attitude to Resolution 242, which obliterates the national right of its people and deals with the cause of the people as refugees. The Council, therefore, refuses to have anything to do with this resolution at any level, Arab or international, including the Geneva Conference.

2. The Liberation Organization will employ all means, and first and foremost armed struggle, to liberate Palestinian territory and to establish the independent combatant national authority for the people over every part of Palestinian territory that is liberated. This will require further changes being effected in the balance of power in favour of our people and their struggle.

3. The Liberation Organization will struggle against any proposal for a Palestinian entity the price of which is recognition, peace, secure frontiers, renunciation of national rights and the deprival of our people of their right to return and their right to self-determination on the soil of their homeland.

4. Any step taken toward liberation is a step toward the realization of the Liberation Organization's strategy of establishing the democratic Palestinian state specified in the resolutions of previous Palestinian National Councils.

5. Struggle along with the Jordanian national forces to establish a Jordanian-Palestinian national front whose aim will be to set up in Jordan a democratic national authority in close contact with the Palestinian entity that is established through the struggle.

6. The Liberation Organization will struggle to establish unity in struggle between the two peoples and between all the forces of the Arab liberation movement that are in agreement on this program.

7. In the light of this program, the Liberation Organization will struggle to strengthen national unity and to raise it to the level where it will be able to perform its national duties and tasks.

8. Once it is established, the Palestinian national authority will strive to achieve a union of the confrontation countries, with the aim of completing the liberation of all Palestinian territory, and as a step along the road to comprehensive Arab unity.

9. The Liberation Organization will strive to strengthen its solidarity with the socialist countries, and with forces of liberation and progress throughout the world, with the aim of frustrating all the schemes of Zionism, reaction and imperialism.

10. In the light of this program the leadership of the revolution will determine the tactics which will serve and make possible the realization of these objectives.

Hamas, on the other hand, was founded in 1987 as a political party by **Sheik Ahmed Yassin** with the primary goal of replacing Israel with an Islamic Palestinian state. Today, Hamas is considered as a Palestinian Islamic organization equipped with a paramilitary force called the Izz ad-Din al-Qassam Brigades. In 2006, Hamas snatched the majority of seats in the Palestinian parliamentary elections and since 2007 Hamas has governed Gaza as a Palestinian territory. Despite being identified as a Palestinian political party, Hamas has garnered notoriety in the international community due to the series of bombings believed to be perpetrated by the Hamas. In fact, the United States, Japan, Canada and the European Union have now classified Hamas as a terrorist organization.

In 1988, Hamas released its charter called the Hamas Covenant in which it calls for the eventual creation of an Islamic state in Palestine and the obliteration and nullification of Israel. Hamas wishes to establish a Palestinian state in the lands that is currently Israel, the West and the Gaza Strip. Given below is the summary of the selected provisions of the Hamas Covenant:[60]

- **Article 1.** It describes the movement's program as "Islam."
- **Article 2.** It defines Hamas as a "universal movement" and "one of the branches of the Muslim Brotherhood in Palestine."

---

[60] Hamas Covenant - http://en.wikipedia.org/wiki/Hamas_Covenant

- **Article 3.** It explains that the movement consists of "Muslims who have given their allegiance to Allah."
- **Article 5.** It demonstrates the Salifist roots and connections to the Muslim brotherhood.
- **Article 6.** It considers Hamas as uniquely Palestinian, and "strives to raise the banner of Allah over every inch of Palestine.
- **Article 7.** It describes Hamas as "one of the links in the chain of the struggle against the Zionist invaders" and links the movement to the followers of the religious and nationalist hero Izz ad-Din al-Qassam.
- **Article 8.** It lays down its slogan of "Allah is its goal, the Prophet is the model, the Quran its constitution, *jihad* its path, and death for the sake of Allah its most sublime belief."
- **Article 9.** It adapts the vision to connect the Palestinian crisis with the Islamic solution and advocates "fighting against the false, defeating it and vanquishing it so that justice could prevail."
- **Article 11.** It regards Palestine as sacred for all Muslims for all time, and it cannot be relinquished by anyone.
- **Article 12.** It affirms that "nationalism is part of the religious creed."
- **Article 13.** It explains that there is no negotiated settlement possible. Jihad is the only answer.
- **Article 14.** The liberation of Palestine is the personal duty of every Palestinian.

- **Article 15.** The Palestinian problem is an Arab-Islamic cause, and Hamas
  deplores the PLO's secular nationalism as a departure from the Arab and Muslim worlds.
- **Article 20.** It calls for action "by the people as a single body" against "a vicious enemy which acts in a way similar to Nazism, making no differentiation between man and woman, between children and old people."
- **Article 22.** It makes sweeping claims about Jewish influence and power reminiscent of the notorious Czarist forgery Protocols of the Elders of Zion.
- **Article 28.** Conspiracy indictment against "Israel, Judaism and Jews."
- **Article 32.** It condemns as co-plotters the "imperialistic powers."

Apart from the PLO and Hamas, there are also political parties which aim at the liberation of the Palestinian people, such as the Fatah, Palestinian People's Party, Democratic Front for the Liberation of Palestine (DFLP), Palestinian Democratic Union, Palestinian Forum, Palestinian National Initiative, Popular Front for the Liberation of Palestine, Al-Mustaqbal and the Palestinian Popular Struggle Front.

17. The Israeli-United Nations Relations

Since the creation of Israel as an independent state in 1948, the United Nations (UN) has issued countless resolutions against Israel. Anti-Israel countries see this as evidence of Israel's bad human rights record while pro-Israel entities view these resolutions to reflect a kind of systematic adaptation and often times recycle admonitions against the only Jewish state in the UN. For example, the former Secretary-General **Kofi Annan** noticed that **"the Council targets Israel in a relentless fashion while rogue states and regimes that systematically abuse human rights are never mentioned."**[61] In this context, it should also be noted that the United Nations Human Rights Council has issued more resolutions against Israel than any other countries combined. It was for such reasons that Secretaries General Kofi Annan and Ban Ki Moon, the European Union, Canada and the United States have accused the council of focusing disproportionately on the Israeli–Palestinian conflict. The United States, therefore, boycotted the Council during the President George W. Bush administration, but reversed its position on it during the Obama administration.[62]

---

[61] Current Realities, Ministry of Foreign Affairs
[62] http://en.wikipedia.org/wiki/United_Nations_Human_Rights_Council#cite_note-6

1. Summary of All UN Security Council Resolutions Adopted Against Israel

From 1955 to 2009 alone, the United Nations Security Council adopted more than 70 resolutions targeting Israel for many violations. These violations have included unlawful attacks on its neighbors, violations of human rights of the Palestinians, deportations, demolition of homes and refusal to abide by the United Nation Charter and the 1949 Fourth Geneva Convention. The United Nations, on the other hand, issued two resolutions seeking peaceful resolution of the Middle East conflict: Resolutions 242[63] and 338.[64] The following is the complete list of all resolutions adopted concerning Israel:

Resolutions	Adopted	Summary
Resolution 106	March 29, 1955	Condemns Israel for Gaza raid
Resolution	January 19,	Condemns Israel for raid on Syria

---

[63] The primary objective of United Nations Security Council Resolution 242 was to end the Arab-Israeli conflict. The resolution was adopted on November 22, 1967, in the aftermath of the Six-Day War. Israel along with Egypt, Jordan, Lebanon, and later Syria agreed to implement Resolution 242 to finally end the Middle East conflict.

[64] The United Nations Security Council Resolution 338 was adopted on October 22, 1973, which called for a ceasefire in the Yom Kippur War in which Israel was attacked by its Arab neighbors, Egypt, Iraq, Syria, Jordan and Libya. The resolution stated that a ceasefire should take place within 12 hours of the adoption of the resolution.

111	1956	that killed fifty-six people
Resolution 127	January 22, 1958	Recommends that Israel must suspend it's 'no-man's zone' in Jerusalem
Resolution 162	April 11, 1961	Urges Israel to comply with UN decisions
Resolution 171	April 9. 1962	Determines flagrant violations by Israel in its attack on Syria
Resolution 228	November 25, 1966	Censures Israel for its attack on Samu in the West Bank, then under Jordanian control
Resolution 237	June 14, 1967	Urges Israel to allow return of new 1967 Palestinian refugees
Resolution 248	March 24, 1968	Condemns Israel for its massive attack on Karameh in Jordan
Resolution 250	April 27, 1968	Calls on Israel to refrain from holding military parade in Jerusalem
Resolution 251	May 2, 1968	Deeply deplores Israeli military parade in Jerusalem in defiance of Resolution 250
Resolution	May 21, 1968	Declares invalid Israel's acts to

252		unify Jerusalem as Jewish capital
Resolution 256	August 16, 1968	Condemns Israeli raids on Jordan as 'flagrant violation'
Resolution 259	September 27, 1968	Deplores Israel's refusal to accept UN mission to probe occupation
Resolution 262	December 31, 1968	Condemns Israel for attack on Beirut airport
Resolution 265	April 1, 1969	Condemns Israel for air attacks for Salt in Jordan
Resolution 267	July 3, 1969	Censures Israel for administrative acts to change the status of Jerusalem
Resolution 270	August 26, 1969	Condemns Israel for air attacks on villages in southern Lebanon
Resolution 271	September 15, 1969	Condemns Israel's failure to obey UN resolutions on Jerusalem
Resolution 279	May 12, 1970	Demands withdrawal of Israeli forces from Lebanon
Resolution 280	May 19, 1970	Condemns Israel's attacks against Lebanon
Resolution 285	September 5, 1970	Demands immediate Israeli withdrawal from Lebanon

Resolution 298	September 25, 1971	Deplores Israel's changing of the status of Jerusalem
Resolution 313	February 28, 1972	Demands that Israel stop attacks against Lebanon
Resolution 316	June 26, 1972	Condemns Israel for repeated attacks on Lebanon
Resolution 317	July 21, 1972	Deplores Israel's refusal to release Arabs abducted in Lebanon
Resolution 332	April 21, 1972	Condemns Israel's repeated attacks against Lebanon
Resolution 337	August 15, 1973	Condemns Israel for violating Lebanon's sovereignty
Resolution 347	April 24, 1974	Condemns Israeli attacks on Lebanon
Resolution 425	March 19, 1978	Calls on Israel to withdraw its forces from Lebanon
Resolution 427	May 3, 1978	Calls on Israel to complete its withdrawal from Lebanon
Resolution 444	January 19, 1979	Deplores Israel's lack of cooperation with UN peacekeeping forces
Resolution	March 22,	Determines that Israeli settlements

446	1979	are a 'serious obstruction' to peace and calls on Israel to abide by the Fourth Geneva Convention
Resolution 450	June 24, 1979	Calls on Israel to stop attacking Lebanon
Resolution 452	November 2, 1979	Calls on Israel to cease building settlements in occupied territories
Resolution 465	March 1, 1980	Deplores Israel's settlements and asks all member states not to assist Israel's settlements program
Resolution 467	April 24, 1980	Strongly deplores Israel's military intervention in Lebanon
Resolution 468	May 8, 1980	Calls on Israel to rescind illegal expulsions of two Palestinian mayors and a judge and to facilitate their return
Resolution 469	May 20, 1980	Strongly deplores Israel's failure to observe the council's order not to deport Palestinians
Resolution 471	June 5, 1980	Expresses deep concern at Israel's failure to abide by the Fourth Geneva Convention
Resolution	June 30, 1980	Reiterates that Israel's claim to

476		Jerusalem is 'null and void'
Resolution 478	August 20, 1980	Censures Israel in the strongest terms' for its claim to Jerusalem in its 'Basic Law'
Resolution 484	December 19, 1980	Declares it imperative that Israel re-admit two deported Palestinian mayors
Resolution 487	June 19, 1981	Strongly condemns Israel for its attack on Iraq's nuclear facility
Resolution 497	December 17, 1981	Decides that Israel's annexation of Syria's Golan Heights is 'null and void' and demands that Israel rescinds its decision forthwith
Resolution 498	December 18, 1981	Calls on Israel to withdraw from Lebanon
Resolution 501	February 25, 1982	Calls on Israel to stop attacks against Lebanon and withdraw its troops
Resolution 509	June 6, 1982	Demands that Israel withdraw its forces forthwith and unconditionally from Lebanon
Resolution 515	July 29, 1982	Demands that Israel lift its siege of Beirut and allow food supplies to

		be brought in
Resolution 517	August 4, 1982	Censures Israel for failing to obey UN resolutions and demands that Israel withdraw its forces from Lebanon
Resolution 518	August 12, 1982	Demands that Israel cooperate fully with UN forces in Lebanon
Resolution 520	September 17, 1980	Condemns Israel's attack on West Beirut
Resolution 573	October 1, 1985	Condemns Israel 'vigorously' for bombing Tunisia in its attack on PLO headquarters
Resolution 587	September 23, 1986	Takes note of previous calls on Israel to withdraw its forces from Lebanon and urges all parties to withdraw
Resolution 592	December 8, 1986	Strongly deplores the killing of Palestinian students at Bir Zeit University by Israeli troops
Resolution 605	December 22, 1987	Strongly deplores Israel's policies and practices denying the human rights of Palestinians
Resolution	January 5,	Calls on Israel not to deport

607	1988	Palestinians and strongly requests it to abide by the Fourth Geneva Convention
Resolution 608	January 14, 1988	Deeply regrets that Israel has defied the United Nations and deported Palestinian civilians
Resolution 636	July 6, 1989	Deeply regrets Israeli deportation of Palestinian civilians
Resolution 641	August 30, 1989	Deplores Israel's continuing deportation of Palestinians
Resolution 672	October 12, 1990	Condemns Israel for violence against Palestinians at the Haram al-Sharif/Temple Mount
Resolution 673	October 24, 1990	Deplores Israel's refusal to cooperate with the United Nations
Resolution 681	December 20, 1990	Deplores Israel's resumption of the deportation of Palestinians
Resolution 694	May 24, 1991	Deplores Israel's deportation of Palestinians and calls on it to ensure their safe and immediate return
Resolution 726	January 6, 1991	Strongly condemns Israel's deportation of Palestinians

Resolution 799	December 18, 1992	Strongly condemns Israel's deportation of 413 Palestinians and calls for their immediate return
Resolution 938	July 28, 1994	Extends mandate of the United Nations interim Force in Lebanon until January 31, 1995
Resolution 1583	January 28, 2005	Calls on Lebanon to assert full control over its border with Israel
Resolution 1701	August 11, 2006	Calls for the full cessation of hostilities between Israel and Hezbollah
Resolution 1860	January 9, 2009	Calls for the full cessation of war between Israel and Hamas

One may wonder whether there have been any resolutions against the Palestinians too. However, it should be noted that as the Palestinian National Authority does not have a permanent diplomatic mission to the United Nations (it only enjoys a permanent observer status, meaning they attend the UN sessions to observe, but not to participate in the sessions or vote on any resolutions), as a non-UN member, the PNA is not subject to any UN Security Council Resolutions.

18. Pro-Israel Organizations

The awareness of the United States government and its peoples' support for Israel as characterized in a variety of ways—such as financial, political, moral and even religious—is beginning to spread like wildfire to all the corners of the world. In fact, there are currently more than sixty organizations that believe and actively advocate Israel's right to maintain a Jewish homeland. Most of these organizations are inspired by the religious fact that no other race is entitled to claim Israel other than the Jewish people because in their view it is enshrined in the Biblical texts. Though the majority of the organizations are based in the United States, there are also other pro-Israel groups in the Netherlands (Christenen voor Israel), Iceland (Zion Vinir Israels) and Spain (Friends of Israel Initiative). Some of the major organizations who support Israel are: Americans for a Safe Israel, Stand with Us, International Fellowship of Christians and Jews, Restoration Israel, The Watchman International, John Hagee Ministries, Messianic Literary Corner, Standing with Israel, Paul Wilbur Ministries and Precept Ministries International.

The following paragraphs provide a summarized account of some of the support in favor of Israel.

a. Christian Zionism

The term "Christian Zionism" was popularized in the mid-twentieth century. The earlier common term was "Restorationism". Christian Zionists believe that the people of Israel remain part of the chosen people of God and also believe that the return of the Jews to the Holy Land, and the establishment of the State of Israel in 1948, is in accordance with Biblical prophecy. It overlaps with, but is distinct from, the nineteenth century movement for the Restoration of the Jews to the Holy Land, which had both religiously and politically motivated supporters.

Many Christian Zionists believe that Jews returning to the land of Israel is a prerequisite for the Second Coming of Jesus. This idea along with the parallel idea that the Jews ought to be encouraged to become Christian, as a means of fulfilling a Biblical prophecy, has been common in Protestant circles of Christianity since the Reformation.

However, not all Christian Zionists believe that Jews must convert to Christianity before the coming of the Messiah[65] and thus don't make the idea of Jews converting to Christianity as a cornerstone for their support. At the CUFI's (Christians United for Israel) 4th annual convention, CUFI Florida state director **Scott Thomas**, who is senior pastor at Without Walls Central in Lakeland, Florida, states that CUFI's support of Israel is not related to Christian eschatology

---

[65] Christians commonly refer to Jesus as either the "Christ" or the "Messiah." Christians also believe Jesus to be the Messiah that Jews were expecting.

since Christians believe that there is nothing they can do to speed up that process. Thomas also cited Chapter 12 of the Book of Genesis, which states that God will bless those who bless the Jews and curse those who curse the Jews, and said that his Christian faith couldn't exist without the foundation of Judaism.[66] Pastor John Hagee, who is the founder and chairman of Christians United for Israel, has stated the following:

> **"Like all people of faith, we Christians firmly believe that our religion is true. But we also believe in religious freedom and have enormous respect for the Jewish faith. The first rule adopted by Christians United for Israel was that there would be no proselytizing at our events. CUFI exists only to honor and support the Jewish people, never to convert them."[67]**

Over the past couple of hundreds of years many evangelists supported and pushed for the return of Jews to the land of Israel. One such prominent figure was **William E. Blackstone** who was an evangelist and Christian Zionist. He initially focused on the Restoration of the Jews to the Holy Land as a prelude to their conversion to Christianity, out of a pious wish to hasten the coming of the Messiah but he increasingly became concerned with the deadly, Russian, government-instigated pogroms and believed that it was necessary to create a Jewish homeland in Palestine. In 1891, Blackstone led a petition drive that was signed by 413 prominent Christian and a few Jewish leaders in the United States. He

---

[66] http://jta.org/news/article/2009/07/23/1006730/cufi-conference-brings-criticism-of-obama-administration
[67] http://cufi.convio.net

personally gathered the signatures of men such as John D. Rockefeller, J.P. Morgan, Senators, Congressmen, religious leaders of many denominations, newspaper editors, the Chief Justice of the U.S. Supreme Court and others. He presented the petition later called the "Blackstone Memorial" to President Harrison in March 1891, calling for American support of Jewish restoration to Palestine.[68]

b. Evangelical Christians and their Support for Israel

Americans in general are known to be more supportive of Israel than any other nation. One of the major indicators of this support has been the financial support that the US has provided to Israel. According to the 2008 Congressional Research Service (CRS) Report, the US has provided $101 Billion in aid to Israel since 1949. The aid has averaged between $2 Billion and $3 Billion yearly for the past few years. This governmental support is also rooted in the backing of some American religious organizations for Israel and the Jews. Among the prominent religious organizations in the United States that express public support for Israel are those of the evangelical Christians.

The evangelical Christians are adherents of evangelicalism, a Protestant Christian theological stream that originated in Great Britain in the eighteenth century as a new breakaway group from Catholicism. As a result of Protestantism's aggressive campaign to

---

[68] http://en.wikipedia.org/wiki/William_Eugene_Blackstone

propagate their beliefs, evangelicalism has spread to all parts of the world. Evangelicalism's key theological beliefs are the following:

- **CONVERSION** – A belief in personal conversion (being "born again")
- **ACTIVISM** – Actively expressing and sharing the gospel[69]
- **BIBLICISM** – A high regard for the supreme authority of the scripture (the Bible)
- **CRUCICENTRISM** – An emphasis on teachings that proclaim the death and resurrection of Jesus

The origin of the word "evangelical" is very Biblical. In fact, evangelicals believe that it has been one of the major themes in the ministry of Christ: to spread the good news. The command to spread the "good news" is written in the Christian text, 1 Corinthians 15:3b-5:

> *"Christ died for our sins according to the Scriptures, that He was buried, that He was raised on the third day according to Scriptures, and that He appeared to Peter, and then to the Twelve (apostles)."*

The etymological origin of the term "evangelical" can be traced to its Greek root *"evangelion"* which means "good news." To be an evangelical Christian, therefore, is to believe in the Gospel of Jesus Christ and spread the good news to all people. Many evangelical

---

[69] A "gospel" is a writing that describes the life, ministry, death, burial, and resurrection of Jesus. The term also refers to the whole New Testament.

Christians define the term "evangelicalism" rather narrowly while others define it very broadly. For instance, more recently, the word "evangelicalism" has become a broader term that describes a movement within the one big umbrella of Protestantism. Therefore, while some evangelical Christians prefer to be identified as Pentecostal Christians, others desire to be labeled specifically as evangelical Christians.

However, it was only in the year 1531 CE that the term "evangelical" was first used by **William Tyndale** (b. 1494 –d. 1536), an English Protestant reformer and Bible translator of the time. A year after Tyndale first used the word in his Protestant writings, **Thomas More** (b. 1478 – d. 1535), an English Catholic philosopher, author and saint, also used the term when he wrote treatises rebutting the Protestant teachings of Tyndale.

The term was used more often during the Protestant Reformation (1517-1648) and every Protestant theologian of the time embraced the term to mean "the gospel truth." **Martin Luther** (b. 1483 – d. 1546), who ignited the Protestant Reformation in Europe in 1517, specifically used the words **evangelische Kirche** or the evangelical church to separate Protestants from the Catholics. The birth of *evangelische Kirche* has brought about national evangelical churches in many European countries, especially in Germany, Denmark and Switzerland. There are also national organizations of evangelical churches in other parts of the world, such as the Evangelical Lutheran Church in America, the Evangelical Church in Germany and the Evangelical Lutheran Church in Canada.

In the United States, three of the most dominant figures responsible for spreading evangelicalism in North America were the English evangelist *George Whitefield* (b. 1714 – d. 1770); *John Wesley* (b. 1703 – d. 1791), the founder of Methodism; and American philosopher and theologian *Jonathan Edwards* (b. 1703 – d. 1758). The missionary efforts of Whitefield, Wesley and Edwards resulted in making evangelical Protestantism to become the most dominant expression of Christianity in the United States in the 1820s. But as millions of non-Protestant immigrants continued to enter the United States in the latter part of the nineteenth and early twentieth century, this dominant religious group in the United States started to dwindle. Despite the influx of non-Protestant immigrants to the United States, however, the evangelical Protestantism remained strongly found in various parts of the country, especially in the south.

During the twenty first century, the term "evangelical" and the concept behind the term has drastically changed and evolved. According to the *Institute for the Study of American Evangelicalism (ISAE),*[70] there are now three major changes in the connotation of evangelicalism.

1. The first major change in the concept of evangelicalism is that Christians who belong to this group believe in the four key doctrines that clearly separate them from others: (a) **Conversionism**, the

---

[70] http://isae.wheaton.edu/

belief that human life needs to be changed; (b) **Activism**, the expression of the Gospel in action; (c) **Biblicism**, a personal regard for the Bible; and (d) **Crucicentrism**, a particular focus on the cross of Christ.

2. The second shift of paradigm is that evangelicalism has become so broad that it now covers other groups, such as the black Baptists and Dutch Reformed Churches, Pentecostals, Mennonites, Charismatic Christians and Baptists.

3. The third major change in the connotation of meaning of evangelicalism in the twenty first century is that it was formed as a coalition of evangelical Christians to combat the fundamertalist movement of the 1920s and the 1930s.

Today, the involvement of evangelical Christians in politics and in other areas of life is undeniably clear. In fact, evangelical Christians have been very vocal in major political issues like the legalization of abortion, capital punishment and same-sex marriage in the United States. They see these issues as against the Biblical teachings of Christ. Today, thirty-seven per cent (37%) of all Christians describe themselves as born-again or evangelical.[71] This puts the number of evangelicals around 92 million (considering that there are about 250 million Christians in the United States).

---

[71] ABCNEWS/Beliefnet poll -
http://abcnews.go.com/sections/us/dailynews/beliefnet_poll_010718.html

c. Religious Reasons for Evangelical Christians' Support for Israel

Unlike other Protestant Christians, the evangelical Christians are passionate about one controversial political issue and that is their support for the Jewish people in Israel. In fact, one of the major aims of Christians United for Israel (CUFI), the largest pro-Israel evangelical Christians' organization in the United States, is **"to communicate pro-Israel perspectives to elected officials."**[72]

The evangelical Christians' support for Israel is based on their Biblical belief that Israel is the Biblical homeland of the Jewish people. The evangelical Christians continue to reecho the call that Israel is the Promised Land given by God to Abraham, Isaac and Jacob during the earliest history of Israel, long before Christianity and Islam were born. The following are the verses from various parts of the Christian Bible (Genesis 15:18-21; 28:13; Exodus: 23:31; Deuteronomy 1:8) that are used in support of this notion:

Genesis 15:18-21; 28:13

It was on that occasion that the LORD made a covenant with Abraham, saying: "To your descendants I give this land, from the Wadi of Egypt to the Great River (the Euphrates), the land of the Kenites, the Kenizzites, the Kadmonites, the Hittites, the Perizzites, the Rephaim, the Amorites, the Canaanites, the Girgashites, and the Jebusites."

---

[72] See "About Christians United for Israel." Christians United for Israel (CUFI), n.d. Web, retrieved on 23 June 2010.

And there was the LORD standing beside him and saying: "I, the LORD, am the God of your forefather Abraham and the God of Isaac; the land on which you are lying I will give to you and your descendants. These shall be as plentiful as the dust of the earth, and through them you shall spread out east and west, north and south. In you and your descendants all the nations of the earth shall find blessing. Know that I am with you; I will protect you wherever you go, and bring you back to this land. I will never leave you until I have done what I promised you."

Exodus: 23:31

I will set your boundaries from the Red Sea to the sea of the Philistines, and from the desert to the River; all who dwell in this land I will hand over to you to be driven out of your way.

Deuteronomy 1:8

"I have given that land over to you. Go now and occupy the land I swore to your fathers, Abraham, Isaac and Jacob, I would give to them and to their descendants."

In the Biblical exegesis, Isaac (Abraham's son) and Jacob (Abraham's grandson), represent the future generation Jews to which the Promised Land (Israel) was to be given as an inheritance. According to the Christian text (Genesis 12:7):

The LORD appeared to Abraham and said, "To your descendants I will give this land." So Abraham built an altar there to the LORD who had appeared to him.

It should be noted that although the Jews claim their closeness to Abraham, Muslims too believe in Abraham. The Quran mentions the following verses:

"Ibrahim (Abraham) was neither a Jew nor a Christian, but he was a true Muslim Hanifa (Islamic Monotheism - to worship none but Allah Alone) and he was not of Al-Mushrikun" (Quran – 3:67).

"Say (O Muslims), "We believe in Allah and that which has been sent down to us and that which has been sent down to Ibrahim (Abraham), Isma'il (Ishmael), Ishaq (Isaac), Ya'qub (Jacob), and to Al-Asbat [the offspring of the twelve sons of Ya'qub (Jacob)], and that which has been given to Musa (Moses) and 'Îsa (Jesus), and that which has been given to the Prophets from their Lord. We make no distinction between any of them, and to Him we have submitted (in Islam)" (Quran – 2:136).

"Or were you witnesses when death approached Ya'qub (Jacob)? When he said unto his sons, "What will you worship after me?" They said, "We shall worship your Ilah (God - Allah), the Ilah (God) of your fathers, Ibrahim (Abraham), Isma'il (Ishmael), Ishaq (Isaac), One Ilah (God), and to Him we submit (in Islam)" (Quran – 2:133).

"And who can be better in religion than one who submits his face (himself) to Allah (i.e. follows Allah's religion of Islamic Monotheism); and he is a Muhsin (a good-doer). And follows the religion of Ibrahim (Abraham) Hanifa (Islamic Monotheism - to worship none but Allah Alone). And Allah did take Ibrahim (Abraham) as a Khalil (an intimate friend)! (Quran – 4:125).

"Say (O Muhammad): "Truly, my Lord has guided me to a Straight Path, a right religion, the religion of Ibrahim (Abraham), Hanifa [i.e. the true Islamic

Monotheism - to believe in One God (Allah i.e. to worship none but Allah, Alone)] and he was not of Al-Mushrikun" (Quran – 6:161).

The efforts of evangelical Christians include spreading the awareness that Israel belongs to the Jewish people and the Jewish people belong to Israel. The evangelical Christians' special affection for the Jewish people is characterized by three important reasons:

1. The evangelical Christians believe that the Jewish people are facing a serious threat of being evicted from their homeland. The Jewish people, therefore, deserve to be supported and protected.

2. They believe that the Bible itself speaks that Israel is the homeland of the Jewish people in perpetuity and therefore they regard this mandate coming directly from God.

3. The evangelical Christians see Israel as a perfect reflection of a democratic United States in contrast to authoritarian and Islamic regimes that continue to claim Israel. (See below for an explanation).

In one of his speeches, Pat Robertson[73] summarized the support of evangelical Christians for Jews as follows:

---

[73] Pat Roberson is a media mogul, television evangelist, ex-Baptist minister and business man who espouses American Christian right political views.

"Ladies and Gentleman, evangelical Christians support Israel because we believe that the words of Moses and the ancient prophets of Israel were inspired by God. We believe that the emergence of a Jewish state in the land promised by God to Abraham, Isaac, and Jacob was ordained by God.

We believe that God has a plan for this nation which He intends to be a blessing to all the nations of the earth.

Of course, we, like all right-thinking people, support Israel because Israel is an island of democracy, an island of individual freedom, an island of the rule of law, and an island of modernity in the midst of a sea of dictatorial regimes, the suppression of individual liberty, and a fanatical religion intent on returning to the feudalism of 8th Century Arabia."[74]

d. Christians United for Israel (CUFI)

In the United States, one of the most active pro-Israel groups that support Israel is the Christian United for Israel (CUFI). The organization provides a national association through which churches, parachurch organizations, ministries, and individuals in America promote pro-Israelism financially and politically. The influence of CUFI is quite vast and its members hold gatherings and summits all over United States in an effort to solicit support from all the Americans and elected officials.

---

[74] Why Evangelical Christians Support Israel - http://www.patrobertson.com/Speeches/IsraelLauder.asp

The CUFI's statement of purpose (www.cufi.org) states the following:

> *"The purpose of Christians United For Israel (CUFI) is to provide a national association through which every pro-Israel church, parachurch organization, ministry or individual in America can speak and act with one voice in support of Israel in matters related to Biblical issues."*

The Christian United for Israel (CUFI) was founded by Pastor **John Charles Hagee** (born April 12, 1940) on February 7, 2006 in the United States to establish a formal group that handles his mission to propagate support for Israel. Hagee has a very deep connection with the political leaders of Israel and as a result has visited the country numerous times. Hagee is also known to have met every Israeli Prime Minister since Menachem Begin. His church, the "John Hagee Ministries", has spent over $8 million to help Soviet Jews return to Israel. Today, CUFI is able to address the United States Congress to defend Israel using the Bible as justification.

John Hagee has openly criticized any Arab claims to Israel. On his website (www.jhm.org), he states the following:

> *"Geopolitically speaking, we should support Israel because it is the only true democracy in the Middle East. The tiny democracy of Israel is surrounded by feudal states and brutal dictatorships that control vast regions of land and oil resources. The presence of the Israeli Defense Forces brings stability to that part of the world.*

The current conflict in the Middle East is not just about land; it's about Israel's right to exist as a nation. The land has never belonged to the people who now call themselves Palestinians. The area was named Palestine by the Romans, but there has never been a nation called Palestine, and there is no Palestinian language. Before 1948 these people were Egyptians, Syrians, Jordanians, Iraqis, and citizens of other Arab nations who had moved to the region. They were displaced by the war of 1948, but Israel is not occupying their territory."

The Christians United for Israel (CUFI) believes that Israel is in peril basically because Iran has threatened to wipe Israel off the map, and so the call to support, protect and defend Israel from nuclear powered Iran is rather an urgent one. In fact, CUFI has designed two objectives related to how the American people can help realize these goals:

a) The Christians United for Israel's (CUFI) primary goal is **"to educate Christians about the Biblical and moral imperatives about supporting Israel."** The first book of the Bible, the Genesis, narrates that Israel is the Biblical homeland of the Jewish people since Abraham and all his descendants received the Promised Land from God himself. The people who believe in the Word of God are morally obliged to follow, implement and realize what the Bible says.

b) The second goal of CUFI is to communicate pro-Israel perspectives to the people, the media and the elected officials of the United States. CUFI believes that though prayer is an effective tool in the realization of this goal, it is however more effective to put the prayer in action and spread the Biblical and moral imperatives to all the people of the world, the media and the United States' elected officials.

The CUFI's support for Israel was recognized by Israeli Prime Minister Benjamin Netanyahu in his welcome speech on Monday March 8, 2010, at a summit of Christians United for Israel (CUFI) in Jerusalem. Netanyahu said:

"Welcome to Jerusalem, the undivided, eternal capital of the Jewish state and the Jewish people. Your presence here today represents a profound transformation in the relationship between Christians and Jews. This transformation has its roots in the 19th century when the early Christian Zionists came to the Land Israel and when they began exploring the land of the Bible, when they began to yearn for the Jewish restoration in this land, the restoration of our numbers, the restoration of our sovereignty. In fact, Christian Zionism preceded modern Jewish Zionism, and I think enabled it. But it received a tremendous impetus several decades ago when leading American clergymen, among them most notably, Pastor John Hagee, a dynamic pastor and leader from Texas, began to say to their congregations and to anyone who listened, it's time to take a stand with Israel. It was time to take a stand with the sole democracy in the Middle East. It was time to take a stand against the lies and the slander and the vilifications. It was time to defend the Jewish state's right to defend itself. Today, Christians, by the thousands, by the tens of thousands, by the hundreds of thousands, by the millions, by the tens of millions - today they have heard this call, and they stand with Israel. I salute you,

the people of Israel salute you, the Jewish people salute you. Time after time, through thick and thin, you have stood shoulder to shoulder with our state, and I have come here tonight to thank you for your unwavering friendship. And today that friendship is more important than ever because Israel faces unprecedented challenges to its security and its legitimacy . . . After centuries in exile, I have come here to assure you, the people of Israel have come home and no force on earth will ever make us leave our home again."[75]

e. Christian Friends of Israeli Communities (CFOIC)

The primary objective of the Christian Friends of Israeli Communities (CFOIC) is to boost the morale of the Jewish people affected by the transfer of territories of Israel to the Palestinian Authority as stipulated in the Oslo Accords in 1993. When the Oslo Accords were implemented, a considerable number of Jewish communities in the West Bank and the Gaza Strip were relocated. The volunteers of the CFOIC provided these Jewish communities with their basic needs as they started a new life as they were relocated in various refugee villages across Israel.

The CFOIC laid out eight Biblical reasons why a Christian should support Israel:

a) Because God says He will bless those who bless them (Genesis 12:3)

---

[75] CUFI Jerusalem Summit 2010 - http://www.cufi.org/

"I will bless those who bless you and curse those who curse you. All the communities of the earth shall find blessing in you."

b) Because we (Christians) owe them a debt for the blessings we have received through them (Romans 9:4-5; 15:27)

> *They are Israelites; theirs the adoption, the glory, the covenants, the giving of the law, the worship, and the promises; theirs the patriarchs, and from them, according to the flesh, is the Messiah. God who is over all be blessed forever. Amen.*

> *[T]hey decided to do it, and in fact they are indebted to them, for if the Gentiles have come to share in their spiritual blessings, they ought also to serve them in material blessings.*

c) Because God's gift and call on Israel have not been revoked (Romans 11:28)

> *In respect to the gospel, they are enemies on your account; but in*

respect to election, they are beloved because of the patriarchs.

d) Because God has promised to bring them back to their land (Amos 8:14)

> *Those who swear by the shameful idol of Samaria, "By the life of your god, O Dan!" "By the life of your love, O Beersheba!" those shall fall, never to rise again.*

e) Because the times of the gentiles are almost fulfilled (Luke 21:24)

> *They will fall by the edge of the sword and be taken as captives to all the Gentiles; and Jerusalem will be trampled underfoot by the Gentiles until the times of the Gentiles are fulfilled.*

f) Because we are to comfort God's people (Isaiah 40:1-2)

> *Comfort, give comfort to my people, says your God. Speak tenderly to Jerusalem, and proclaim*

> *to her that her service is at an end,*
> *her guilt is expiated; Indeed, she*
> *has received from the hand of the*
> *LORD double for all her sins.*

g) Because we must make reparation for anti-Semitic teachings and acts.

h) Because God is working with them to work out his plan for world peace (Romans 11:15)

> *For if their rejection is the*
> *reconciliation of the world, what*
> *will their acceptance be but life*
> *from the dead?*

The CFOIC was founded by Sondra Oster Baras, who was born in Cleveland, Ohio. Baras was educated in the United States, but later she decided to settle down in Israel along with her family. The CFOIC has offices in Germany, Holland, the United Kingdom, South Africa and Bulgaria.

f. Friends of Israel

In other parts of the world, the call to support, protect and defend the existence of Israel as the Jewish homeland in Palestine is also getting heard. In Spain, former Spanish Prime Minister **Jose Maria Aznar** (1996-2004), along with other influential figures in Europe and around the world, has founded the Friends of Israel to express his support for the people of Israel. The political background of Aznar as the former Spanish Prime Minister renders the Friend of Israel a political group, as compared to many pro-Israel groups which are religious in nature.

The Aznar call to support Israel is merely a reiteration of the United States commitment to Israel, that is, the rightful recognition of Israel as the Jewish state in the Middle East. But one of the unique pronouncements of Aznar about Israel is the emphasis on the Judeo-Christian roots of Israel which has inspired not only the Catholic Spain, but all the predominantly Christian countries around the world. Aznar, who is a Catholic, believes that *"the assault on Israel is an assault on the Judeo-Christian values."*

Though the basis of Aznar's call to support Israel is rooted in his religious belief, the political ingredient of the call is without a doubt the most dominant of all. In fact, it is clear in the Friends for Israel's objectives, entitled "Stand for Israel, Stand for the West," that Aznar is primarily concerned about Israel as a state:

a) To combat the de-legitimization of the State of Israel at home, abroad and inside the institutions of the international community.

b) To publicly show our solidarity with Israel's democratic institutions – the legitimate expression of the Jewish people's millennial aspiration to live in peace and freedom in its national homeland.

c) To support Israel's inalienable right to secure borders unmolested by terrorists or tyrannical regimes so that its citizens can continue living with the same guarantees that our own societies enjoy.

d) To consistently and firmly oppose the prospect of a nuclear armed Iran.

e) To work to ensure that Israel is fully accepted as a normal Western country, an essential and indivisible part of the Western world to which we belong.

f) To reaffirm the value of the religious, moral, and cultural Judeo-Christian heritage as the main source of the liberal and democratic Western societies.

Along with Aznar, the other founders of the Friends of Israel are George Weigel, former Peruvian president Alejandro Toledo, philosopher and former president of Italian senate Marcello Pera, Irish politician and Nobel Peace Prize laureate David Trimble, British historian and writer Andrew Roberts, United States Permanent Representative to the United Nations ambassador John Bolton, former Spanish Minister of Industry Carlos Bustelo, international French financier Roberto Agostinelli and Italian politician Fiamma Nirenstein.

--- The End

19. Appendix I: About the Religious Scriptures

This section provides a short introduction to the religious texts of the three religions of Judaism, Christianity, and Islam.

a. Jewish Scripture

The **Tanakh** is a name used in Judaism for the canon of the Hebrew Bible. The name is an acronym formed from the initial Hebrew letters of the Jewish text's three traditional subdivisions: The **Torah**, **Nevi'im** ("Prophets") and **Ketuvim** ("Writings") — hence **TaNaKh**. The Christians refer to Tanakh as the *Old Testament*.

1. **Torah** literally means "teaching" or "law" and is composed of Five Books of Moses whose names are *Bereshit* (Genesis), *Shemot* (Exodus), *Vayikra* (Leviticus), *Bamidbar* (Numbers) and *Devarim* (Deuteronomy). The Torah is the first of three parts of the Tanakh (i.e. Hebrew Bible), the founding religious document of Judaism.

2. **Nevi'im**, which means "prophets," is composed of 19 books: Joshua, Judges, Samuel, Kings (I & II), Isaiah, Jeremiah, Ezekiel, Hosea, Joel, Amos, Obadiah, Jonah, Micah,

Nahum, Habakkuk, Zephaniah, Haggai, Zechariah and Malachi.

3. **Ketuvim**, which means "writings," is composed of 11 books: Psalms, Proverbs, Job, Song of Songs, Ruth, Lamentations, Ecclesiastes, Esther, Daniel, Ezra-Nehemiah and Chronicles.

The **Talmud** is a central text of mainstream Judaism, in the form of a record of rabbinic discussions pertaining to Jewish law, ethics, philosophy, customs and history.

b. Christian Scriptures

As explained previously, the Christians inherited the entire Hebrew scripture (*Tanakh*) and baptized it with the name Old Testament or the collection books written before the birth of Christ. The New Testament,[76] a collection of books written after the death of Christ and which the Jews never came to recognize, is, therefore, unique to Christians only. The New Testament is composed of 27 books:

[76] The authorship of the books of the New Testament, which was written after the death of Christ, is attributable to the very names of the books, like the four Gospels which were written by Matthew, Mark, Luke and John. The apostle Paul is the author of other books, such as the Letters to the Romans, Corinthians, Galatians, Ephesians, Philippians, Thessalonians, Letters Timothy, Titus, Philemon and James. The apostle Peter is the author of the books named after him, First and Second Epistles of Peter. Finally, the apostle John is believed to be the author of the Book of Revelations.

1. Gospels according to Matthew,
2. Mark
3. Luke
4. John
5. Acts of the Apostles
6. Epistle to the Romans
7. First Epistle to the Corinthians
8. Second Epistle to the Corinthians
9. Epistle to the Galatians
10. Epistle to the Ephesians
11. Epistle to the Philippians
12. Epistle to the Colossians
13. First Epistle to the Thessalonians
14. Second Epistle to the Thessalonians
15. First Epistle to Timothy
16. Second Epistle to Timothy
17. Epistle to Titus
18. Epistle to Philemon
19. Epistle to the Hebrews
20. Epistle to James
21. First Epistle of Peter
22. Second Epistle of Peter
23. First Epistle of John
24. Second Epistle of John
25. Third Epistle of John
26. Epistle of Jude
27. Epistle of Revelation

Finally, with respect to the Christian Bible, there are also various translations from the Greek (Septuagint) and Latin (Vulgate) versions. Among the famous English Christian Bible translations are Douay-Rheims (Old Testament, 1582; New Testament, 1609-1610, Catholic translation), Revised Standard Version (King James Version (1611, Protestant), New American Bible (1970, Catholic translation) and New International Version (1978, Protestant translation).[77]

c. Islamic Scriptures

In Islam, there are two sources of divine knowledge –

Quran – Quran is the word of God (Allah) that was revealed to Prophet Muhammad. In Islam, Quran is a continuation of God's message for mankind that was revealed in Jewish and Christian texts. However, according to Islamic beliefs, as those texts and teachings were corrupted by people over time, Quran as the word of God (Allah) was revealed to refresh Allah's message for mankind. In Islam, therefore, while Muslims are supposed to recognize Torah and Bible as Jewish and Christian texts that were revealed by Allah,

---

[77] The Christian doctrine of Biblical inspiration teaches that the books of the Bible were written by human hands which were handed down from generations to generations. Though the writers were humans, they were nevertheless inspired or guided by God (*theopnuestos*) as they wrote the Word of God. As a result of this doctrine, both the Catholic and Protestant scholars agree that the Bible is the Word of God and is therefore infallible, though they differ in opinion and interpretation of some texts in the Bible.

Muslims are not supposed to follow those teachings as the word of God was changed. Instead, Quran is the ultimate authoritative religious text for Muslims.

Hadith are narrations and traditions of Prophet Muhammad that Muslims are supposed to abide by as part of their daily lives. In many cases, these narrations are also a further explanation of the message of the Quran. The six major Hadith collections include the following: Sahih al-Bukhari, Sahih Muslim, Sunan Abu Dawood, Al-Sunan al-Sughra, Sunan al-Tirmidhi and Sunan ibn Majah. Sahih al-Bukhari and Sahih Muslim are considered the most reliable of these collections.

20. BIBLIOGRAPHY / REFERENCES

- "About Christians United for Israel." Christians United for Israel (CUFI), n.d. Web. 23 June 2010.
- "Al-Aqsa Guide." Friends of Al Aqsa, n.d. Web. 27 June 2010.
- "Al-Aqsa Mosque." Wikipedia, n.d. Web. 27 June 2010.
- "Al-Aqsa Mosque in Jerusalem." Al-Aqsa Islamic Society, n.d. Web. 27 June 2010.
- Aznar, Jose Maria. "Jose Maria Aznar: Supporting Israel." Aish, n.d. Web. 23 June 2010.
- Aznar, Jose Maria. "Stand for Israel, Stand for the West." Friends of Israel Initiative, n.d. Web. June 23, 2010.
- "Aliyah." Wikipedia, n.d. Web. 26 June 2010.
- "Aliyah: the Word and Its Meaning." The Jewish Agency for Israel (JAFI), n.d. Web. 26 June 2010.
- "A List of United Nations Resolutions Concerning Israel." Wikipedia, n.d. Web. 22 June 2010.
- "Aliya." Wikipedia, n.d. Web. 21 June 2010.
- "Arab-Israeli Wars." The Columbia Electronic Encyclopedia, n.d. Web. 20 June 2010.
- "British Mandate: 1920-1946." The Jewish Agency for Israel (JAFI), n.d. Web. 20 June 2010.
- "Basilica of the Annunciation, Nazareth." Sacred Destinations, n.d. Web. 27 June 2010.
- "City of David." Wikipedia, n.d. Web. 27 June 2010.
- "Church of the Annunciation." Wikipedia, n.d. Web. 27 June 2010.
- "Church of the Holy Sepulcher." Wikipedia, n.d. Web. 27 June 2010.
- "Church of the Holy Sepulcher, Jerusalem." Sacred Destinations, n.d. Web. 27 June 2010.
- "Church of Maria Magdalene." Wikipedia, n.d. Web. 27 June 2010.
- "Church of Mary Magdalene, Jerusalem." Sacred Destination, n.d. Web. 27 June 2010.
- "Church of the Nativity." Wikipedia, n.d. Web. 27 June 2010.

- Crusader Art is the Holy Land, From the Third Crusade to the Fall of Acre, 1187 – 1291, Jaroslav Folda, 2005
- "Crusades." Wikipedia, n.d. 13 July 2010.
- "Camp David Accords." Israel Ministry of Foreign Affairs, 17 September 1978. Web. 22 June 2010.
- "Camp David Accords." Wikipedia, n.d. Web. 22 June 2010.
- "Christianity and Judaism." Wikipedia, n.d. Web. 9 July 2010.
- "Defining Evangelicalism." Institute for the Study of American Evangelicals, n.d. Web. 11 July 2010.
- Defining the Term in Contemporary Time." Institute for the Study of American Evangelicals, n.d. Web. 11 July 2010.
- "Dome of the Chain." Wikipedia, n.d. Web. 27 June 2010.
- "Dome of the Chain, Temple Mount, Jerusalem." Sacred Destinations, n.d. Web. 27 June 2010.
- "Dome of the Rock." Encyclopedia Britannica, n.d. Web. 27 June 2010.
- "Dome of the Rock." Wikipedia, n.d. Web. 27 June 2010.
- Durand, Alfred. "Inspiration of the Bible." The Catholic Encyclopedia. Vol. 8. New York: Robert Appleton Company, 1910. Web. 18 July 2010.
- Dolphin, Lambert. "The Temple of Solomon." Temple Mount, n.d Web. 9 July 2010.
- "Early History of Jerusalem." Palestine Facts, n.d. Web. 25 June 2010.
- "Evangelicalism." Wikipedia, n.d. Web. 11 July 2010.
- Freund, Michael. "Because the Bible Says So." Free Public, 23 September 2002. Web. 23 June 2010.
- "Geneva Accord." Wikipedia, n.d. Web. 22 June 2010.
- "Greater Israel." Wikipedia, n.d. Web. 12 July 2010.
- "Greater Israel Movement." Encyclopedia of the Middle East, n.d. Web. 12 July 2010.
- Gottheil, Richard et al. "Jerusalem." Jewish Encyclopedia, n. d. Web. 19 June 2010.
- Hanson, Victor Davis. "Why Support Israel?" Aish, n.d. Web. 23 June 2010.
- Herzl, Theodor. The Complete Diaries of Theodor Herzl. New York: Herzl Press and Thomas Yosecoff, 1960. Print.
- "History of Jerusalem." Wikipedia, n.d. Web. 19 June 2010.
- Israel 1967-1991: Sabra and Shatilla. "What Happened at the Sabra and Shatilla Refugee Camps in 1982." Palestine Facts, n.d. Web. 9 July 2010.

- "Israel." Wikipedia, n.d. Web. 21 June 2010.
- "Israel-Jordan Peace Treaty." Israel Ministry of Foreign Affairs, 24 October 1994. Web. 22 June 2010.
- "Israel Labor Party Definition." Zionism and Israel-Encyclopedic Dictionary, n.d. Web. 21 June 2010.
- "Israeli-Jordan Peace Treaty." Wikipedia, n.d. Web. 22 June 2010.
- "Israeli Political Parties." BBCE News, 5 April 2006. Web. 20 June 2010.
- "Israeli Political System and Parties." Zionism and Israel-Encyclopedic Dictionary, n.d. Web. 20 June 2010.
- Jacoby, Jeff. "Why are Americans so pro-Israel?" Aish, n.d. Web. 23 June 2010.
- "Jerusalem and Islam." Jerusalemites, n.d. Web. 27 June 2010.
- "Jerusalem in Islam." Wikipedia, n.d. Web. 27 June 2010.
- "Jerusalem in Judaism." Wikipedia, n.d. Web. 27 June 2010.
- "Jerusalem: The City of David." Jewish Virtual Library, n.d. Web. 27 June 2010.
- "John Hagee." Wikipedia, n.d. Web. 24 June 2010.
- "Jesus." Wikipedia, n.d. Web. 11 July 2010.
- "Jesus Last Days in Jerusalem." Jesus in Jerusalem, n.d. Web. 9 July 2010.
- "Jerusalem at the Time of Christ." Bible History, n.d Web. 9 July 2010.
- "Kataeb Party." Wikipedia, n.d. Web. July 10, 2010.
- "Kadima." Wikipedia, n.d. Web. 21 June 2010.
- Kreeft, Peter. "Comparing Christianity and Judaism." Catholic Education Resource Center, n.d. Web. 9 July 2010.
- Lazarte, Alan C., B.A., LL.B. "The Biblical Reasons for Christian Support of Israel." Christian Action for Israel, n.d. Web. 23 June 2010.
- "List of English Bible Translations." Wikipedia, n.d. Web. 12 July 2010.
- "Likud Definition." Zionism and Israel-Encyclopedic Dictionary, n.d. Web. 21 June 2010.
- "List of Political Parties in Israel." Wikipedia, n.d. Web. 21 June 2010.
- Lorch, Netanel. "The Arab-Israeli Wars." Israel Ministry of Foreign Affairs, 2 September 2003. Web. 25 June 2010.

- Mark, Clyde R. "Israeli-United States Relations." Policy Almanac, 17 October 2002. Web. 22 June 2010.
- Mathias, Elliot. "Israel Wants Peace." Aish, n.d. Web. 23 June 2010.
- McGrath, Alister. Evangelicalism and the Future of Christianity. InterVarsity Press, 1995. Print.
- Meranda, Amnon. "Olmert: Only delusional fantasists believe in 'Greater Israel.'" Ynet News, 26 May 2008. Web. 17 July 2010.
- "Middle East." Wikipedia, n.d. Web. 21 June 2010.
- "Mount of Olives." Wikipedia, n.d. Web 27 June 2010.
- "National Union (Israel)." Wikipedia, n.d. Web. 21 June 2010.
- Netanyahu, Benjamin. "National Security." Netanyahu, n.d. Web. 20 June 2010.
- "Oslo Accords." Wikipedia, n.d. Web. 22 June 2010.
- "Pro-Israel Organization." International Wall of Prayer, n.d. Web. 24 June 2010.
- "Promised Land." Wikipedia, n.d. Web. 24 June 2010.
- "Permanent Mission of Israel to the United Nations." Israel-United Nations, n.d. Web. 25 June 2010.
- "Qadima (Kadima) Party." Zionism and Israel-Encyclopedic Dictionary, n.d. Web. 21 June 2010.
- "Reasons Why a Christian Should Support Israel." Christian Friends of Israel Communities (CFOIC), n.d. Web. 23 June 2010.
- "Religious Significance of Jerusalem." Wikipedia, n.d. Web. 27 June 2010.
- Robertson, Pat. "Why Evangelical Christians Support Israel." Pat Robertson, n.d. Web. 23 June 2010.
- "Sabra and Shatila Massacre." Ynet News, 1 August 2006. Web. 10 July 2010.
- "Sabra and Shatila Massacre." Wikipedia, n.d. Web. 10 July 2010.
- "Tanakh." Wikipedia, n.d. Web. 9 July 2010.
- "The Importance of Jerusalem in Judaism and Israeli History." Zionism-Israel, n.d. Web. 25 June 2010.
- "Torah." Wikipedia, n.d. Web. 9 July 2010.
- "The Balfour Declaration of 1917." Wikipedia, n.d. Web. 19 June 2010.
- The New American Bible originally published in 1969 by Thomas Nelson, Inc.

- "The United Nations: II. The Balfour Declaration." Palestine Remembered, n.d. Web. 19 June 2010.
- Soufan, Saira W. "Meaning of Jerusalem to Islam." Jerusalemites, n.d. Web. 27 June 2010.
- "Temple Mount." Wikipedia, n.d. Web. 27 June 2010.
- "The Importance of Jerusalem in Judaism and Israeli History." Zionism-Israel, n.d. Web. 27 June 2010.
- "The Western Wall." Jewish Virtual Library, n.d. Web. 27 June 2010.
- "What Was The British Mandate?" Palestine Facts, n.d. Web. 20 June 2010.
- "What is an Evangelical?" Grace Communion International (GCI), n.d. Web. 9 July 2010.
- "What is Evangelicalism?" Got Questions, n.d Web. 9 July 2010.
- "What is the Difference Between Christianity and Judaism?" Got Questions, n.d. Web. 9 July 2010.
- "World Zionist Organization (WZO)." Jewish Virtual Library, n.d. Web 19 June 2010.
- "Western Wall." Wikipedia, n.d. Web. 27 June 2010.

Other Books by IqraSense.com

1. Jesus – The Prophet Who Didn't Die
2. Summarized Stories of the Quran
3. The Power of Dua (Prayers)
4. Inspirations from the Quran - Selected DUAs, Verses, and Surahs from the Quran: Includes Select Commentary, Tafsir, and Reasons for Revelation
5. Healing and Shifa from the Quran and Sunnah
6. DUAs for Success
7. And more

ABOUT THE AUTHOR

IqraSense.com is an Islamic blog covering religion topics on Islam and other religious topics. To discuss this topic in more detail, you are encouraged to join the discussion and provide your comments by visiting the blog.

Printed in Great Britain
by Amazon.co.uk, Ltd.,
Marston Gate.